From the Heart

a collection of columns by

Ginger Hutton

Golden West Publishers

Back cover photo: Mike Fioritto

Cover design: Bruce Fischer/The Art Studio

The chapters in ***From the Heart*** were published originally in ***The Arizona Republic,*** and have been edited by Ginger Hutton for this collection, reprinted with permission of ***The Arizona Republic.***

Library of Congress Cataloging-in-Publication Data

Hutton, Ginger
From the heart.

I. Title.
PN4874.H86A25 1987 814'.54 87-25136
ISBN 0-914846-33-7

Dedication

For Joe, my love

Foreword

For twelve years Ginger Hutton has had an ongoing love affair with her many readers. One would think that after so long a time, it would have cooled off—but, like a good marriage, it has matured with age. Mainly, there are two reasons for this:

First, there is mutual respect. Ginger shares her life experiences with the readers who share theirs with her. When she does move into controversial subjects, it is to explore the personal relationships involved, not for the sake of controversy. It becomes a learning experience for both—and the reader never feels "used."

Second, Ginger has avoided the trap which columnists and TV personalities sometimes fall into—that of becoming experts in all areas of human relationships. It is especially dangerous if the self-anointed authority has some sort of a degree, thereby adding credibility to the advice. There are no pat answers to psychological problems.

This is Ginger Hutton's third book—and it is her best.

For those of you who have not read her columns in the *Arizona Republic,* I would suggest that you read the prologue first because it will give you some insight about the author. I have found, too, that one of the charms of this book is that it need not be read in chronological order. Just open it anywhere and start reading. You will feel as though you've invited a friend into your home.

Nicholas P. Dallis, M.D.

Dr. Dallis is a psychiatrist and author of the comic strips "Rex Morgan, M.D.," "Apartment 3-G" and "Judge Parker," distributed by the News America Syndicate.

Contents

PROLOGUE

The old woman you see is not me. The wrinkles webbing pictures in my face, the graying, yellowed hair are not what I am.

I am mother, wife, daughter, sister, friend. I am a woman who knows how to run an office and a home, who knows the poetry of Wordsworth and the essays of Emerson. I am a woman who lost a son in childbirth and another in the war.

I am a child who skated down sidewalks and got up again when I fell because the flying was worth the fall. I am a teenager who danced and dreamed and fell in love.

My age is part of me because it testifies to all the years I've lived and learned. But please don't see just the body that is wasting away.

Please see all that I have been and am. Please see ME.

• • •

The fat man you see is not me. The sagging body that cannot fit into airplane seats comfortably, the broad hips and heavy arms that cause people to stare and whisper. They are not me.

I am a child who grew up loving the out-of-doors, spreading my arms into the wind as I ran, feeling God in mountains and trees.

I am a man who stops to pick up injured dogs on the street and pays the veterinary bills. I am a father who hurts when his daughter doesn't make the gymnastics team or his son has a fight with his best friend. I am the husband who worries about losing his wife to someone more handsome, more successful.

The fat is part of me because it is my challenge, and so it colors my life and personality as I fight it. But it is only a tiny particle of what I am.

Please don't judge me by my girth. Look into my eyes and see ME.

• • •

The handicap you see that makes you look past me as though I don't exist. . .it is not me.

I am a woman who loves and longs to be loved. I watch the couples in the store shopping for groceries together and I dream of shopping with someone whose smile warms my heart. I watch the children play and my arms ache for one of my own.

My handicap is part of me because I have had to make peace with it. And in doing so, I've made peace with the less obvious handicaps of other people, like resentment, prejudice, hate.

I understand frustration and hopelessness better than anyone and I know the subtle ways they can cripple a life. So I try not to overreact when people treat me as if I were not quite a person, as if I were not all there.

But I AM here, just as surely as you are.

Please look through my misshapen coat of flesh and see ME.

• • •

The skin color you see is not me. It is only nature's adaptation to the sun and was not meant to be a curtain between us. We have made it so.

I am not all those things you have been told or have read about my race. I am me.

I am the man who loves the feel of the earth in his hands as he plants the beginning of a flower. A man who counts the stars at night with his children and answers their questions about life and loving.

I am the man who gets up early to go to work and

comes home late to worry about his wife's health and his son's homework.

I am the child who didn't know he was different until someone told him.

My difference from you is part of me because it has molded my life in some ways, but it is only an illusion we have created together.

Can you see past the difference? Can you see ME?

● ● ●

Can you see that, what I am, you are, too? Can you look deep enough into our hearts, our minds and our souls to discover we are sisters and brothers? Can you understand that we are more alike than we are different? That we share the same fears of rejection and ridicule, the same hopes for success and happiness, the same need for love?

Please see ME. I'm trying my best to see YOU.

Chapter 1

So this is love!

Love, look what we've found.
We have found the secret
So many lovers have been searching for...

The bride's aunt sang the song she had written, while in the lobby her niece waited nervously for the moment when she would move down the aisle to change her name and her life.

The groom was nervously waiting to make his entrance, too. The day before, he had stopped by when the bride and her relatives were decorating the church reception hall with white bells and pink crepe paper.

"This is your last chance to back out," his future wife teased him. "No way!" he responded, giving her such a loving look that those watching nearby looked quickly away.

The young man and woman had done all the traditional things: the bachelor party, the wedding shower. They had made the difficult decisions: who would be best man and maid of honor, who would be attendants, what friends would be left off the wedding list because their families are so large there wouldn't be room for everybody.

Despite some minor disagreements between relatives, the weeks of planning had gone quite well. The bride and her mother talked with pleasure about the arrangements, and about the past and future, when they went out to breakfast together the morning of the wedding.

Afterward, the daughter wrote a letter to her mother:

Even though I have lived separate from you for some time now, I feel today like I'm leaving you for the first time. . . . Maybe getting married makes being an adult more official. I am now going to have my own family.

Please remember, Mama, that I love you so much . . . and all the sweet memories you have given me.

She was indeed grown up and beautiful in white lace and ruffles, her mother's necklace around her neck, her great-grandmother's handkerchief in her sleeve, and excitement and hope in her eyes and her smile.

The tiny flower girl, dark-haired and dark-eyed in white lace, marched solemnly down the aisle to where her uncle waited to greet his bride. The bridesmaids followed. Then the maid of honor.

The crowd rose. The bride floated on the music to her future husband, who stepped down to meet her and escort her up the steps. Then he held her hands and sang a Freddie Jackson song, never taking his eyes from hers:

You are my lady.
You're everything I need and more
You're all that I am living for . . .
Our love will shine;
Let's make it last until the end of time.

Friends and relatives who had not begun crying during the first song were bringing out handkerchiefs now. Even the minister brushed back tears.

After the second song, and a poignant moment in

which it appeared the bride and groom were going to kiss before the traditional time, the minister spoke:

One of the beautiful things about marriage is that while two lives unite to become one, you do not thereby become less yourselves, but more . . . for in this union there is true freedom, not possessiveness.

Yes, they said, they would love, comfort, honor, cherish and remain faithful to each other. Finally, they kissed. Then, joyously, they hugged each other twice.

The triumphant march back down the aisle was followed by loving congratulations from friends and family, picture taking and the traditional sharing of the first piece of cake. He got frosting on her nose; she smashed cake into his mustache.

Later, at a dinner outdoors at the home of the groom's family, the newlyweds danced, their arms tightly wound about each other. Around and around they danced, in a world of their own, as the full moon shone and a soft breeze lifted her dress and veil.

And so on Aug. 16, my daughter, Kimberly Rose Hutton, became Mrs. Jose Luis Martinez. A wife. Close to someone else's heart.

But she is still in mine, too. And always will be.

I've been thinking about what I would expect if I were getting married again. And drawing on what the years have taught me about love, marriage and the idiosyncracies of even the most ideal mate, I would make a different set of marriage vows than I did years ago.

I would say:

I promise, my love, to understand that you will not be strong all the time nor have all the answers or do all the right things. I know you are a complex person, with weaknesses as well as strengths, and there will be times when the weaknesses overcome you and the strengths fail you, and you will need me to be strong, to find answers and to understand.

I promise not to get so hung up on little things like toothpaste tubes squeezed in the middle and clothing discarded on the bathroom floor that I forget all the important things like tenderness and humor that made me want to marry you.

I will also try to live as comfortable as possible with my own imperfections because I know that to love you I have to love myself. If I have learned to forgive myself for being human, then I can forgive you for being human.

I promise to have children only after we really know each other and have put down roots strong enough to survive the upheaval that children can bring to a marriage. Then I promise to work with you, not against you, as we raise them so they will know their lives are securely grounded in our love.

I promise to know you'll change and to help you make those changes so you can feel good about growing. And because both of us will change, I understand the love we have now will not be the same love we have 10 years or 20 years from now because we will not be the same people. I know our love will not only be different, but deeper.

I promise to forgive and forget the times you have hurt me and to not bring them up again later to win a quarrel. I know that when one of us wins a quarrel, the other has to lose and feel bad. The only way to really win is to reach lovingly past our differences toward each other so no one loses.

I promise to be honest with you about my feelings and my needs. I will not play games. But I will not let honesty get in the way of compassion, so that I feel compelled to "honestly" hurt you when a kind word will make you feel better.

I recognize that one of the deepest needs of human beings is to overcome separateness, but with the meeting of that need comes responsibility. If you freely give me so much of yourself that we sometimes feel as one, then I must treat what you have given me carefully. I will not turn your secrets against you in anger or discard our closeness should someone at the office appear momentarily tempting.

I promise to listen to you, to respect you, to understand that you have needs I may not have, because you are different from me. Just because I don't have the same needs doesn't mean yours aren't valid.

I promise to value the pleasure and help you give me, and to return help and pleasure to you. And when you can no longer be of help or pleasure because you are in emotional or physical pain, I'll take care of you because I love the person you are.

I promise to be your lover, your partner, your lifelong friend.

* * *

The woman said she felt much better about her marriage since she gave up her expectations.

"I had this idea about how a man should be—how a husband should be," she said. "A man was supposed to always be the aggressor sexually. The woman was supposed to be talked into sex, not have to talk him into it.

"It is not the way with Roy and me at all. I usually initiate sex.

"For a while I really let that bother me—that he didn't get the idea before I did. I built it up in my mind, even considered looking for someone else who would pursue me. Then I started thinking about how he was immediately in the mood when I suggested it, and he's romantic and loving then.

"And I also thought about all the other good things we share. And I decided to be glad he was easy to turn on and to quit worrying about whose idea it was first."

A man made a similar adjustment in attitude. He learned to accept the idea that his wife was never going to be the stay-at-home mother and wife that his mother had been. He grew up expecting to marry someone who would take care of him, his house and his children while he earned the living and went out with the guys.

Instead, he married a woman who wanted a career, believed housework and child-rearing should be shared by husband and wife, and felt she deserved as much freedom in her life as he had in his.

"It was really hard at first," he said. "We fought a lot. But I've come to realize that that is the way she is, and it isn't necessarily wrong. And I love her, so I have to let her be the way she needs to be. I still get mad sometimes, but now I just figure that's my problem and I work it out by myself."

Both of these people have realized that in a successful relationship, you learn to accept things the way they are and people the way they are. And they are seldom exactly the way we think they should be.

We all grow up with ideas of "supposed to" behavior. Men are supposed to be a certain way; women are supposed to be a certain way. If you love someone, you're supposed to say certain things, do certain things. And if you don't, you are not a "real" man or a "real" woman, or you aren't "really" in love.

The reality is that a spouse is not likely to fit our image of what he or she "should be." In particular, a spouse is not likely to fit the image of the perfect person romantic novels tell us we should get for a mate.

For instance, a woman who thinks men should "take charge" has been happier in her marriage since she has realized it is all right for her to be the decision-maker. "I used to wait around for him to decide where we were going to eat," she said. "And as he vacillated, I got mad until the evening was ruined for both of us. Now I decide where we're going to eat and call and make the reservation. And we're both happy."

A marriage counselor has remarked to a woman that her husband "has an absolute right to be what he wants to be. And you have an absolute right to decide whether you want to live with it."

It sounds at first as if he is giving her permission to quit on the marriage, but that's not what he's saying. He's stating the fact that it's impossible to change someone else. They have to want to change themselves.

So if her husband doesn't want to change, she could decide to leave him. She could also decide to change her attitude. She could give up demanding that he fit her idea of what a man or husband should be.

Once she realized that no person is going to be her idea of a "perfect" man and no relationship is going to be "perfect," she found there was enough worthwhile in the relationship to make it worth hanging onto.

As another woman, in similar circumstances put it: "I realized I wanted Mark to fit the image of 'husband.' I had to give up 'husband' and love Mark."

* * *

Two women were discussing how their husbands agree that they should help around the house, but they really don't want to do it. Yet, if their wives get tired of waiting for their help and do a job themselves, they get angry.

"We were going to clean out the spare room this weekend," one woman said. "He kept putting it off and putting it off. Finally, I couldn't stand it. I did it. Then he felt guilty about it and got mad at me."

Guilt seems to be a major motivator for some men struggling with the new roles and rules for husbands. A man told me when he gets home from work and hears his wife trying to get supper while dealing with fussy kids in the kitchen, he knows he should help, but he doesn't want to.

"I sit there thinking I should give her a hand but don't want to. I feel guilty because I know she's having a rough time and needs it.

"But my mother did it all by herself—my father didn't help. So I resent doing it."

Lately, he said, the guilt gets to him more than the resentment, so he goes out and helps.

One young career woman said she resents it that her husband doesn't help do more of the household chores. She also resents the word "help."

"It's his house, too, but it's as if he's doing me a favor when he 'helps' me with the housework," she said.

The women complain that even the husbands who are "helping" feel they have the right to choose not to do certain things. They might agree to vacuum, for instance, but not do dishes.

Men and women admit that part of the problem is some men don't know how to do housework chores the way the women want them done.

"I was used to just throwing all my clothes in together and washing them," one man told me. "My wife was furious when I did her laundry that way. She said I ruined her blouses."

They finally compromised: He mops and waxes floors, and she does the laundry.

Young couples who have worked out good arrangements tell me they don't worry about what is a woman's job or a man's job. Many of them live in apartments and have their automobiles fixed by mechanics, so the so-called man's jobs—lawn, automotive and household repair—don't exist.

In one family, the husband cooks and cleans up most meals. The wife does all of the laundry and ironing. They shop for groceries together. She cleans the bathroom, he vacuums and makes the bed.

"We didn't sit down and decide this," she said. "It just sort of evolved."

Another woman decided early in her marriage that she was not going to be in the kitchen before and after dinner the way her mother was, while the rest of the family was having fun in the living room.

Shortly after the honeymoon, she was cleaning up after supper one evening when she asked her husband: "Are you going to help me?"

"I wasn't intending to," he replied.

She was first surprised, then angry. She let the matter rest for a few days while she tried to figure how to deal with it. She knew her husband's mother had done everything around the house.

Finally, she explained to her husband that if he helped, they could spend more time together. She could watch TV with him the way he wanted her to, instead of having to be in the kitchen all the time.

He accepted this argument, reluctantly at first, but it soon became part of their routine to get dinner together, eat dinner together, clean up together and watch TV together.

"I didn't want my kids to grow up thinking that only a woman cooked and did dishes," she said.

"I wanted them to grow up knowing that you help when other people need help—you don't have silly rules like, 'I won't do that; it's a woman's (or a man's) job.' You do it because the person needs your help, and it's the nice thing to do."

Now, she, her husband and their two little boys help before dinner and after. They also all help out in the yard. It's accepted that when something needs to be done, everyone "helps."

* * *

The moon was big and yellow in the eastern evening sky. A breeze stirred the trees and filled the night with the sweet scent of flowers.

But the couple didn't notice. They were arguing as they walked.

"It's cold out here," he said, hugging his arms against the jacket of his warmup suit. "I thought winter was supposed to be over."

"Cold?" she said. "This isn't cold. It's just nice."

"Your thermostat is off," he said. "It's cold."

"It is not," she said. "You're the one who's off . . ."

A nice evening, another special moment spoiled by a common human problem: the inability to recognize that each person is different. Each individual reacts to things differently for a number of reasons: upbringing, physical makeup, mood at that moment. But we tend to see the disagreement not as an issue of difference but as one of right and wrong.

And we have to prove ourselves right because if we agree the other person might have a point, that would make us, heaven forbid, wrong.

This need to be right extends to the most inconsequential things in our daily lives. Besides whether the weather is comfortable or not, other silly things I've heard people debate include:

- Whether it's healthier to sleep in a cold room or a hot room.

- Whether steaks are better for you rare or well-done.
- Whether putting cream in your coffee is bad for you.
- How often a normal individual should have to go to the bathroom (a popular traveling argument).
- How soon after dinner should you need to stop to get something to drink.
- How soon after dinner you should be hungry again.
- Whether the toothpaste should be curled from the bottom or squeezed wherever you feel like it.
- Whether toilet paper should roll out from under or out from over.
- Whether sugar gives you energy or makes you sleepy.
- Where the pans should be kept in the kitchen.
- Whether it's better to wash clothes in hot or cold water. (He says it is easier on the clothes if they are washed in cold; she says they don't get clean.)
- Whether a living room with some books, clothes and toys lying around looks "messy" or simply "lived in."
- Whether it is necessary to make the bed every morning, since you are just going to get back into it again that night.
- Whether all the shirts in the closet should hang with collars facing the same way.
- Whether canned goods should be kept in alphabetical order or medicines should be arranged according to bottle size, with labels showing.
- Whether you'll catch cold if you go without your jacket or get your feet wet on a cool day.
- Where you should sit in a movie theater to make it easier on your eyes.

Most of these discussions would be easily solved if the people involved would just say "I prefer to sit here" or "I prefer my coffee with cream." But we love to make it a moral issue, to argue it—and to win.

Unfortunately, when we win, someone we love loses. And a beautiful night, or moment, can slip by unnoticed.

* * *

The nice things we say are important in a relationship, but even more important is what we learn not to say.

For instance, a woman told me that after years of trying to tell her husband to be more careful about his driving, she realized she wasn't solving driving problems, she was creating marriage problems. Every vacation trip they took was ruined by fights about whether he was following too closely or not changing lanes when he should.

The last few years she kept her mouth shut, and they've had a much better time. "I realized he wasn't going to drive any differently, no matter what I said. So I just try to watch the scenery and not think about it. We've both been happier."

She's learned one of the conversational rules for a healthy relationship: Don't mention something that will cause trouble and won't change anything.

Some other conversational don'ts include:

● Don't mention things your spouse can't change. For instance, a man I know told his wife: "You're starting to get lines around your eyes. What happened?"

It would have been OK for him to remark that she should change her lipstick or her blouse, but she can't help getting older. His remark made her feel ugly.

● Don't nag about things he's wrestling with, like stopping smoking or giving up hot fudge sundaes. He's already feeling bad about himself; it doesn't help to know that you don't like him, either.

● Don't repeat bad things other people have said about her. It will just make her feel awful and create more problems.

● Don't say critical things about your spouse in front of your friends. A woman once said to a friend of mine: "I wish Ron had your talent for fixing things; he can't change a light bulb." Everyone laughed, but her husband looked most uncomfortable.

A lot of people say hurtful things in front of others without realizing what they are doing. They may see the flaw as minor and are just joking about it, as was the woman about the light bulb.

However, I've met some people who will argue for the truth, no matter what. They claim the adage "if you can't say anything nice, don't say anything at all," is dishonest. An honest person will say exactly what he thinks, no matter how much it hurts someone else.

And they further justify it by saying: "He needs to know," or "Well, she should just change then," or "Nobody can hurt your feelings unless you let him."

Nonsense. We have a responsibility not to unnecessarily harm anyone in any way.

Of course, there are times when it is necessary to tell a loved one about something that is bothering us. Then, careful timing is important.

For instance, don't tell him what he's doing wrong when you are making love. Bring it up later, when you're talking and feeling good about each other.

Don't tell her you hate her haircut; she can't do a thing about it now. Wait until it grows out, then say, "I like it better long."

Loving someone is learning when to say some things and when not to say anything at all.

* * *

He was wondering, said a friend, how to explain to his fiancee that he needed a lot of time alone.

"I love her," he said, "but I don't seem to need as much togetherness as she does. In fact, last weekend after we were together for several days, I was beginning to feel very antsy. I wanted her to leave for awhile."

We talked then of why we liked to be alone at times and how it was difficult for us to understand people who have to be at a spouse's elbow every moment or who don't like to do anything without a friend along.

I like to shop by myself, go to classes by myself and sometimes attend meetings by myself because when you're part of a couple, you are a closed group. When you're alone, you're open to other people.

After a class or meeting, I like to exchange ideas with strangers, then take those conversations back to someone I love.

In the grocery store I like to watch people, the old woman carefully comparing prices or a young couple awkwardly trying to please each other with their choices. "Do you like pork chops? No, if you don't like them very much we can have something else."

In the cashier's line recently, a woman good-naturedly told me about the problems she's having adjusting to her college daughter returning home. And an older man described some of the problems he'd encountered while driving to Phoenix from New York. Neither would likely have talked with me if I had been in line with a friend.

We needed time alone to think, too, my friend and I agreed. I said I'd found that if I don't get enough undisturbed time to sort through things that are bothering me, to make decisions and set goals, I become emotionally off-balance.

But I like only a few hours to myself, I added, then I need people again or I'll go crazy from solitude, too.

He said he could use days of aloneness, especially outdoors in the wilderness. There he can put long strings of thoughts together—something he could never do in the city because of interruptions.

He also notices things like cloud shadows on mountains, the sounds of birds and animals that he wouldn't notice if he were absorbed in another person. And he sometimes feels as if he were kin to nature, one with the plants, mountains, sky and animals.

I understood that, I said. As much as you love another person, you can't acquire that intense personal relationship with nature when they're there. It's as if three's a crowd.

He felt that way gardening, too, he said. He liked it to be just him and the earth and plants.

"But," he said, laughing, "when I'm done, I want her to come see what I've planted. I want to share it then."

We agreed that the two needs were strong—the need for someone to love and share with, and the need for time to yourself. But it's a rare loved one who can understand that the phrase "I need to be alone," is as simple a statement as "I need to eat."

It is not saying "I don't love you."

* * *

A woman watched a co-worker's pleasure at receiving an anniversary bouquet of roses from her young husband. Then she remarked ruefully to a friend that in 20 years of marriage, she and her husband had never given each other a gift or card.

"We decided we didn't need to buy each other things to prove we loved each other," she said. "But now I'm wondering if we made a mistake."

She and her husband were having problems, and

she was examining all the things she thought could have gone wrong.

"I think the problem is that we've not had any great things happen in our marriage recently," she said. "There's been nothing to make us feel really good about each other or our future together."

Her friend listened, then said, "I don't think it's the big, exciting things that make a marriage work. I think it's the little things."

Then she talked of her own 24-year marriage. She and her husband had been through serious financial problems, an adolescent son who gave them problems, parents who tried to split them up. But through it all, they had a secure sense that their love for each other had an undercurrent strong enough to carry them through anything.

"And I think the reason we've always felt that way is that we're always thinking of each other in little ways," the woman said. "For instance, I'll be busy in the kitchen and George will come in and say, 'Put down those things and come watch the sunset with me,' and I'll say, 'But dinner will be late.'

"And he'll say, 'Let dinner be late.' And we'll watch the sunset with our arms around each other, and when we come back in the house we're feeling so close—just because we took a few minutes to share a sunset."

The other woman nodded. "That's nice," she said, "but do you think it's really necessary to give gifts on Christmas or Valentine's Day? My husband says he's not going to give a card just because Hallmark tells him to."

The woman replied she thought unexpected gifts on any day were wonderful, but those on expected days were great, too.

"There have been times when I was feeling a little

provoked at George, and then I'd get a Valentine card or a birthday card from him, and he'd edit out the parts he didn't like and added thoughts of his own, and all of a sudden I'd forget why I was mad at him and love him so much again."

But she also likes the spontaneous gifts, she admitted.

"Sometimes, when he knows I'm having a bad day, George will leave a little stuffed animal or a note on the bedroom pillow, or I'll find my favorite candy bar wrapped with red ribbon in the refrigerator."

She added that it wasn't just the gifts, either.

"It is all the little thoughtful things he does—remembering to pick up the chips I like when he stops for some for himself," she said. "The way he comes in and tucks me in when I'm lying down for a nap, or the way he fixes green chili burros for lunch when a friend of mine is over to visit so I won't have to cook.

"And he has called every afternoon of our marriage, just to talk a minute even though we're going to see each other a few hours later."

She also felt the fact that both of them cleaned up, complete with cologne, for each other before going to bed added to the romance.

"I think looking nice for your husband and wife says you think they're worth a little extra trouble," she said. "Each time you go out of your way a little for your husband or wife, it says 'I'm thinking of you and you're important to me.' When you both feel that special, I don't think there is anything your marriage can't survive."

* * *

They'd had an early dinner out and weren't ready to go home yet, so he suggested they drive to the top of

South Mountain to watch the sunset.

"That'd be nice," she said, smiling.

But after they passed the park entrance and started toward the mountain, she noticed the gas tank was nearly empty.

She hesitated. He was always certain they could go miles with the warning light on. She had a choice of worrying throughout the drive or making him aggravated at her. She chose the latter.

He argued first that they'd have plenty of fuel, then turned around. A mile or two out of the park they found a service station and filled up.

He hadn't seemed angry, but when they got back in the car, he turned toward home rather than the mountain.

"Aren't we going up the mountain?" she asked.

"It's too late, now," he responded.

She sat in silence, her anger building as he drove home. Finally, she could stand it no longer.

"Well, that was really childish," she said. "Getting even with me for asking you to get gas by not going up the mountain."

"I wasn't getting even," he said. "It was too late to drive up."

"Don't give me that," she said. "You know you were getting even."

He didn't say anything. They drove home in silence, and when they arrived, she went into the bedroom.

On the dresser were the roses he'd surprised her with earlier in the week. She lay across the bed, looking at the roses and thinking how little she knew this man she'd been married to for only a few months. He could be so considerate and then do such stupid things as get even because she'd wanted to get gas.

It had started to be such a romantic evening. They should've been standing on the mountain now, arms about each other, looking at the city lights. Instead, she was alone in the bedroom and he was in the living room.

She could stand it no longer. She went to the living room and asked him why he hadn't driven up the mountain.

"I really thought it was too late," he said. "I'd been uncertain about being up there too long after dark anyway, but thought if we hurried, we could watch the sunset and then come right back down again.

"When we turned back, I expected it would be a while before we'd find gas, so I'd already given up the idea of driving up there. I assumed you had, too. I didn't realize you were angry until you said something."

"And I assumed we were going to get gas so we could go up the mountain," she said.

"You should have said you still wanted to go," he said. "Surely you don't think I'm so childish as to get even with you."

"I've known some men who would have," she said. "I should've known better, but I assumed that's what you were doing."

He laughed and hugged her. "I think we'd better do a little less assuming and a little more talking to each other from now on," he said.

* * *

If you like sex, read.

If you don't like sex, read.

If you believe everyone naturally knows how to make love and shouldn't have to study how to do it, read anyway. You will be surprised at the hang-ups and misconceptions you developed as you were growing up.

For some reason, we take it for granted that we need to study to become experts in other areas of our lives, such as in engineering or cooking. But when it comes to making our relationships work, we think we should automatically know it all. Admitting we need help in raising children or making love is tantamount to saying we were born genetically defective.

When I was 18, I thought my parents had told me everything about sex until a close friend married and told me about her bedroom activities. Some of them shocked me.

"I know," she said. "But you'll find when you get married, your husband will ask you to do a lot of strange things, too."

Since that time, I've realized that the things she had labeled as "strange" were healthy heterosexual activities that are enjoyed by most couples. But I didn't automatically know that; I had to learn about "natural" sex from my friends and husband and books.

For instance, in her book *For Each Other,* Lonnie Barbach discredits the myth of "normal" sexual desire—popularly thought of as the desire for sex several times a day if you are a "real man" and not too often if you are a "real lady."

"A 1972 study showed that the average person has sex approximately two times a week, and the frequency generally decreases with age," writes Barbach, author of several books on sexual problems.

"However, it is important to remember that a national average is precisely that—an average," she adds. "Millions have sex more frequently and millions have sex less frequently. What one person considers a lack of interest is quite normal interest for another person."

The problem arises when one partner (not always the man) in a relationship wants sex more often than the other partner. Barbach tries to help people reconcile those differences and live more happily together.

A friend of mine told me he thought people read too much about sex and feel like failures when the books make them believe they have to reach impossible pleasure goals.

Some books may do that, but most books about other people's sexual needs or problems make us feel better about ourselves and our loved ones. We discover we—and they—are not so strange after all.

"But if you love someone, you're not going to worry about doing something that you think is strange," my friend argued. "You want to do what makes the other person happy. You don't have to read to know that."

Unfortunately, a lot of people love deeply, but they also have deeply ingrained feelings about what is "right" or "wrong" that keep them from expressing it the way their mates want them to. They need help to overcome those inhibitions.

Loving does not mean you have to know everything about making love or that you will no longer have hang-ups. It simply means being willing to try to overcome those hang-ups in order to meet the reasonable requests of a partner.

It could mean going to a counselor or reading a good book.

* * *

Three women—one married, one engaged, one living with a man—talked about when they knew they had really made a commitment.

When they started living together, she thought of it as "trying it out" to see if they could get along well enough to get married.

Everytime something went wrong, she would think, "I don't have to live with that. If he doesn't shape up, I'm leaving." When things went right, she would think, "I really love this man," and she would bring up the subject of marriage during dinner.

But then they would disagree on a political issue and she would think, "We're not going to make it. I should be looking for someone who thinks more like I do."

She had one foot in and one foot out of the relationship, just as she had some of her things in her house and some in his house. But, gradually, as she moved more of her possessions—her books, records, furniture—into his house, she moved into the relationship more emotionally, too.

"When I realized I was committed to him was one day when I was mad at him for something he was doing and I realized I was not thinking about leaving," she said. "I was actually thinking about how I was going to get through this bad time of his until we could be happy again."

She felt fine about being with him until they became engaged. Then she panicked. It was her second marriage and she didn't want another divorce. The wedding date loomed like the gate to a prison: She had better like what was on the other side of the walls because she was going to be forced to stay there.

So now, every incident in their relationship became a test question: Did they measure up on sexual compatibility? Was she going to be able to live with his inability to fix anything mechanical? Would he be able to live with her bad moods?

She was looking at things with such a critical eye that she could see nothing but flaws. And one day, a happily married aunt pointed that out.

"No person and no relationship is perfect," the aunt said. "If you want to marry him, you have to have some faith in him and yourself that you'll be able to solve the problems and get through the hard times together."

After the talk with her aunt, the woman decided to quit looking for trouble and concentrate on wedding plans. Something surprising happened.

"I started seeing again all the special things about my fiance," she said. "I saw what a good man he was, and one day I felt so good because I realized I felt peaceful about getting married. I knew we were going to make it because we really loved each other."

Through the four years of their up-and-down marriage, she knew divorce was a way out if she wanted it. Everytime she got angry or depressed over something he did, she thought about it. Then he became seriously ill.

"Immediately I thought, no, this can't be true," she told a friend later. "I don't want anyone else. I want this man! He's got to get well."

He did, and their marriage is in its 15th year.

What these three women recognized was that there comes a moment in solid relationships when you realize you love this person—that you aren't going to walk out on him or her, no matter what happens, just as you wouldn't walk out on other people you love, like your children and your parents. It's in that moment, married or not, that you are really married.

Chapter 2
Who put the "sin" in single?

The poor guy on the telephone probably didn't expect to get landed on verbally, but I couldn't help it.

He was easily the 10th person I had heard from in the last week who told me he or she didn't go to single dances or answer singles ads in newspapers because everyone at the dances or in the ads had to be "losers."

This man had called in response to a letter from a woman in my column. She was divorced after 25 years of marriage and wrote poignantly of loneliness and longing for the right man. "I just haven't found the bush he is hiding under," she said.

The man had phoned hoping to meet that woman. "Nice men aren't hiding under bushes," he said. "We're out here hoping to meet nice women, but where are they?"

His words echoed those in a letter I received the same day from a man who also said the men the women were looking for weren't hiding under a bush.

"They are right in plain sight. They are not riding on a white horse dressed in shining armor. Nor do they hang out in bars or nightclubs.

"Instead they are working at jobs in industry and offices. They are looking for women just like those that you wrote of.

"But where are the women you talk about? How can we find them? But most important, how do we get acquainted without being looked upon as being 'on the make'?"

Ah—I love that term: "on the make." I've heard it over and over again as an explanation for why people don't go to singles clubs, singles dances, etc. "Everyone there is 'on the make.' "

The man on the phone said that was why he didn't answer singles ads, also. "Those women are obviously on the make," (I suggest everyone who is looking for a relationship is on the make—including him.)

He also doesn't try to meet women in church groups. "I go to church to worship God, not meet someone." And he doesn't attend meetings of singles organizations. "I don't have the time."

And he listed all his career and home obligations.

"What you're saying," I told him, "is that you don't want to make the effort to meet someone. You want some perfect person to conveniently land in your lap without you going out of your way.

"The fact is," I continued, "the reason all you nice men and women don't get together is that you've decided not to. You've decided not to go to places where singles meet. And you use all these excuses about the people at these places being 'losers' to justify your lack of action."

I don't minimize the problems of meeting and I know a lot of excuses made by single men and women cover up feelings of insecurity. I also realize that if you are not gorgeous and getting older (especially women), you suffer rejection more often.

The man on the phone described some of the "losers" as not being good looking, while he described himself as "nice appearing."

Pardon my indignation, folks. But looks don't make the loser or winner. Nor does a singles dance. Nor does a singles ad.

And, while I still intend to do articles on how singles can meet at a later date, I have one suggestion right now:

Get out and meet people. Advertise, dance, go to church, go to parties, go anywhere other singles are. And get rid of all those snobbish stereotypes you've drawn of people you don't know.

Look at it this way: If all you "winners" get out to the places you've said the "losers" are, there'll be a lot more winners there.

* * *

The woman and her 32-year-old son were having problems with the idea that every year is leap year now.

"I just can't get over girls these days," said the woman, shaking her head as her son talked about his difficulties in dealing with the women who called him, left him notes, asked him out. Despite how pleasurable it might sound to someone whose phone isn't ringing, he disliked having to say no.

"I hate to hurt anyone's feelings," he said. "It was easier when I just did the asking."

It was easier in some ways. In the past, men only had to deal with the problem of refusing dates for such special occasions as the Sadie Hawkins Day dance. And while women had permission to ask for dates for those events, they often were uncomfortable.

For instance, one woman told me she and her cousin used to ask each other's dates to the leap year dance, so if the guy said no, they wouldn't feel as bad.

Even though men and women now have received society's permission to ask or refuse any time, they still often are not comfortable with it and sometimes develop silly new rules.

One man told me it was OK if a woman asked him out to lunch, but she better not ask him out for dinner. How is any woman supposed to know his particular boundaries?

It seems so much more reasonable to forget artificial rules and treat our friends of the opposite sex as honestly as we do friends of the same sex.

For instance, a woman will say to another woman when they discover they both like Woody Allen: "Why don't we go see his new picture Friday night?" Why not do the same thing with a male friend?

Actually, it surprises me that so many women who control other aspects of their lives have trouble taking the initiative in dating. They hold down professional jobs, contact clients, make sales, run business meetings. They hire household help, organize the children, lead neighborhood projects and raise money for charities.

However, when it comes to romance, they revert to passive games of "trying to let him know I'm available so he'll notice me and ask me out."

They even panic when a stranger shows interest in a safe setting. For instance, a woman I know saw "the best looking man" in a grocery store a recent Sunday afternoon. He found her attractive, too, and introduced himself. However, she was so locked into the old idea that a woman should not encourage strangers that she panicked and discouraged him.

The next morning, she told friends at work that she

could kick herself because he had seemed so nice. "But I just didn't know what to do," she said.

What she could have done was give him a business card and ask him to call her at work. Then she could have set up a meeting in a neutral, public place like a coffee shop.

She hadn't realized that today it's OK for women to encourage strangers carefully and that many people meet in such everyday places as the supermarket or laundry.

It also is OK today for a woman to:

- Write a man a note suggesting that she would like to go out with him and include her phone number.
- Ask him to meet for coffee, lunch or a drink after work.
- Simply say, "Why don't we go to the Suns game Saturday night? I'll get some tickets."

As for rejection, men have survived it for years. Women are capable of doing it, too.

* * *

It makes me sad, sometimes, to read my mail. Recently it has been full of letters from women in their 40s and 50s saying they can't find men interested in women their ages.

Then I hear from men saying they are lonely, too—that women aren't interested in caring, good men. The women they meet want rich men or are hooked on abusive ones.

I know they are both right to some extent.

I read the singles ads and see men asking for women much younger than they are.

I listen to radio date-lines and hear the man trying desperately to make what he does for a living sound financially attractive. He knows that if he has just an ordinary job, she is going to say "Dump him."

I hear women advise other women not to go out with men who are too old because they may not be able to perform in bed or because they soon will need a full-time nurse.

I hear men remarking about "menopausal" women or saying, as one did to another who was engaged to a woman older than 40: "Why do you want to marry her? She's only got a few good years left."

Add to this the people who don't go anywhere because they figure they will find "only losers" at singles activities, and I begin to wonder how anyone gets together. We put so many roadblocks in our way.

When a man and a woman do meet, they are both self-conscious, knowing everything about them is being scrutinized, from the cleanliness of their fingernails to the part of their hair.

It is difficult to be yourself under such circumstances. A man or a woman who can be fun when comfortable can be stiff and do everything wrong when meeting someone for the first time.

"No way am I going out with that clod," said one woman after her luncheon date with a man who spilled his water all over the table and remained flustered throughout the lunch.

It is difficult to win on first meeting: Both people have built up expectations, basing their judgment on how he sounded on the phone or how she was described by a friend.

So a woma goes to meet Tom Selleck and finds Danny DeVito. Or a man hoping to meet Suzanne Pleshette finds someone who looks like the shy woman who served him hot dogs at the airport.

If either is disappointed because the date doesn't fit the picture he or she composed, it requires a lot of effort to get past that disappointment and see anything to like.

Then, take the matter of self-confidence, which is the most attractive garb a person can wear. It is difficult to be self-confident when you have found out too often that you are too old, too fat, too poor, too something to suit the people you are meeting. So your nervousness makes you less attractive.

Most of us have had the experience of learning to like someone we work with. Had we met him through an ad or on a blind date, we probably would not have given him a second chance. But as we get to know him, he becomes more and more attractive.

One woman I know, who is happily married, said she was turned off at first by the fact that her future husband was so overweight. But they kept running into each other—he was good friends with a friend's husband—and she began appreciating his humor, kindness and intelligence so much that she agreed to go out with him.

Then one day she found she was physically attracted to him, something she thought would never happen with a fat man.

Men and women alike, we set outselves up for disappointment when we take a list of requirements with us to meet someone. Let us try giving everyone we meet at least a second chance.

Perhaps someone nice will be smart enough to do us the same favor.

* * *

My friend came into the office one morning and sat silently at her desk, sipping coffee and staring glumly at the small spot of desk visible through stacks of papers, mail and magazines.

She was so unlike her usual cheerful self that I asked her what was the matter.

"Nothing," she said, bursting into tears.

A few moments later, in the privacy of the lounge, she confessed.

"I've got to stop it," she confessed, raining tears onto the back of the vinyl couch. "I can't take it anymore. The pain isn't worth it."

"What are you talking about?" I asked. "What have you got to stop?"

"Matchmaking," she replied. "I'm always getting people together, and it always turns out disastrously. I just matched up one of my best friends with a nice guy at church. He took her out a couple of times and then broke her heart. She was on the phone last night crying her eyes out.

"Now I hate myself for getting her involved. Why, oh why, can't I quit matchmaking?"

I knew just how she was feeling. I had been through similar matchmaking experiences a thousand times.

First, there is the wonderful, romantic high you get when you have just gotten two nice people together. You have changed their worlds, you have written them a happy ending. You feel powerful—you are a benevolent partner with God.

But then, inevitably, there is the comedown. It did not work. You failed again. The high was only temporary.

You tell yourself one more time that happiness cannot be found in making matches. You will never do it again. Ever.

But then you see someone you know would be perfect for your brother, and you cannot stop yourself. You show her his picture, you show him her picture. You tell her how nice he is, you tell him how much she likes to hike—just like he does.

You feel this surge of urgency; you have to get them together. You ask him whether he has called her yet. You ask her whether she would like to join you and your brother for lunch.

Finally, they meet. They go out two times, three times. Then there are problems.

Oh dear. What if your friend gets hurt? What if your brother gets hurt? You keep asking them how it is going. You keep trying to figure ways to patch it up. It is taking a lot of your time and energy. It is no longer fun. "Why did I ever get into this?" you ask yourself. "I don't want to be responsible for someone being hurt."

So a few weeks later, when you meet a wonderful man at a party, you tell yourself that it is none of your business that he is the perfect age for this nice woman in the office. You remind yourself how awful a matchmaking hangover can be.

But insidiously undermining your willpower is the memory of that one success years ago, when you introduced two friends and they fell in love. You were maid of honor at their wedding. As you held their firstborn in your arms, you thought: "I started all this. I did it."

Suddenly, you just have to have that sense of power again. The need to make a match overwhelms you. You approach the attractive woman in the office. "I know this man . . .," you say.

Anyone out there interested in forming a matchmakers anonymous group? Call me; my friend and I are desperate.

* * *

The men and women were shaking their heads over the recent marriage of two teenagers because the bride was pregnant.

"When something happens, it is always the girl's fault," one woman said. "The girl is the one who is supposed to maintain control. You can't blame the boy."

I could not believe I was hearing that statement in this supposedly enlightened day, but then I thought of something I had read recently.

In the book *Raising a Child Conservatively in a Sexually Permissive World,* authors Sol and Judith Gordon wrote:

"It is important for parents to understand the tremendous pressure on teenage girls to have sex. Boys use lines.

"A recent study conducted by Planned Parenthood in Chicago surveyed a thousand young men. They were asked if it was OK to lie to a girl, to say that you were in love with her in order to have sex. Seventy percent said yes!"

I also remembered that just a few years ago, a man I knew told me that he had lied about loving women many times to get them to do what he wanted them to do, and he felt no guilt about it.

"It's up to her to say, 'No,' if she doesn't want to," he said. "It's always been that way."

What he was saying is that the rules of the dating game make it perfectly all right for a man to use any dishonest tactic he can. If the woman cannot resist such lines as, "I love you; if you really loved me, you'd do it," she's a bad woman. She wears the scarlet A, while he was just being a man, after all.

I had hoped such perverse thinking had gone out with some other crazy men-women games of the 1950s, but apparently it hasn't.

The big argument for the girl setting the limits has been that the boy's sexual desire is stronger, and the girl is the one who suffers the consequences: pregnancy.

There are two major myths here. First, innumerable sex manuals will tell you that a lot of women have stronger sexual desires, and a lot of men do not. So it is not always true that the boy simply cannot control himself, and the girl can.

The other myth is that the girl is the only one who pays for irresponsible sex. The boy often suffers, too. He may end up getting married long before he is ready. Or, if not, he can be told by the court to help support his child.

Besides accepting responsibility for his actions, the boy needs to protect himself. A girl may get pregnant on purpose to make him marry her.

This happened with one man I know, who thought the woman was on the pill. He didn't marry her, but he is now paying support for his child.

But the main reason for boys and girls, men and women, taking equal responsibility for what happens in the dating and mating game is that it is the right and loving thing to do.

You do not trick somebody into having sex or into getting married by being dishonest. That is using another person for your own purposes without thought of his or her welfare.

It is cruel and wrong and not something a "real" man or woman would do.

* * *

In the movie *The Buddy System,* a boy accuses his mother of not being able to make anyone love her.

She replies that it is not her job to make someone love her, and when he asks what love is, she answers: "I don't know. I just know it's not a trick."

Ah, that's a revelation! You would judge by the

things we say, do and watch on television, that most of us define love as a trick.

We can trick people into loving us by the cologne we wear, the shaving utensils we use, the jewelry we give them.

We can trick them with food. If we prepare it just right and present it romantically, we can trick them into wanting to eat that way for life.

A lot of experts are willing to teach us the tricky road to love. They present classes in flirting and write books on how to catch a man or woman.

However, most of us learned the tricks by osmosis. When I was growing up, both girls and boys knew that the way to catch a member of the opposite sex was by pretending to be what we were not. Girls pretended to be weak and to like everything the boys liked. Boys pretended to be better, smarter and stronger than they were.

Girls were great at arranging chance meetings to trick boys into asking them out. They happened to be walking past the classroom every day at the time his class let out or just happened to need a ride home from a club meeting.

Many a situation comedy has been written about boys who asked friends to play *Cyrano* and win a girl to their cause or who developed stories of wealth and daring to get girls interested in them.

Actually, we played the worst tricks on ourselves. We saw someone's laughing eyes or alluring walk and decided that if they had those wonderful attributes, they must, indeed, have all the other qualities wonderful people have. We looked at them and saw not what they were but what we wanted to see.

It was a cruel trick on the ones we fell in love with, too. No wonder they are hurt when we express our disappointment. No wonder they say, "But you knew the way I was. Why does it bother you now?"

The biggest trick we played on ourselves was believing that love is that wonderful, mesmerizing exhilaration we feel when we first dissolve in the arms of an attractive man or woman.

M. Scott Peck, psychiatrist and author of the book *The Road Less Traveled,* writes that the misconception that falling in love is love has caused a lot of problems in marriage.

He says, "The experience of falling in love is specifically a sex-linked, erotic experience." And he adds that it has little to do with loving. "The experience of falling in love is invariably temporary. No matter whom we fall in love with, we sooner or later fall out of love if the relationship continues long enough."

However, he adds that when a couple falls out of love, they may begin to really love.

Peck defines love as an act of will. We don't fall in love. We choose to love. We overcome our fears of vulnerability and our laziness and decide to do loving things for the other person even when we're tired, irritable or the other person is being particularly unlovable.

We make a commitment to them to treat them lovingly, to not do anything to hurt them and to do everything we can to help them.

When we keep that loving commitment to someone, he says, it is strong enough to outlast a lifetime of temptations to succumb again to the tricks of falling in love.

* * *

If you're looking for love outside yourself, you're looking in all the wrong places.

Erich Fromm, in *The Art of Loving,* says you must

first develop a deep love of life and people—then love will come to you. People are always attracted to people who are having a great time doing a lot of things.

"Being fully awake. . . and, indeed, not to be bored or boring is one of the main conditions for loving," writes the psychoanalyst. "To be active in thought, feeling, with one's eyes and ears throughout the day. . . is an indispensable condition for the practice of the art of loving."

We're fooling ourselves if we think we can separate romantic loving from the rest of our lives, he says.

"If to love means to have a loving attitude toward everybody, if love is a character trait, it must necessarily exist in one's relationship not only with one's family and friends, but toward those with whom one is in contact through one's work, business, profession," Fromm says.

Having that loving attitude toward everything and everyone will help when you meet that blind date, too. You will give him or her another chance—even if he is overweight, even if she did dye her hair green by accident.

And you will decide ahead of time that you will enjoy the meeting, whatever happens, because you like meeting people of all kinds.

But if you're desperate to meet someone, you're not likely to be asked to dance. Desperation says you can't be happy by yourself, you have to feed off someone else's happiness, and that's frightening. No one wants to be trapped into being another person's permanent life preserver.

If you love yourself and are enthusiastic about life—if you really like people—it will show in the way you look and the way you act. Chances are you will be asked to dance all evening—perhaps even for a lifetime.

Chapter 3
Changing loves, changing lives

It was a miracle wrought by the occasion. Years of bitterness between the former husband and wife were washed away at their daughter's wedding.

The mother had been apprehensive the weeks before the ceremony, as she helped her daughter prepare. After all, she had been warned by friends to prepare for the worst.

She heard stories of former husbands who would not pay wedding expenses, who refused to wear what they were supposed to, who sulked throughout the reception. She heard of relatives who vented their bitterness, about new wives who were uncomfortable and let everyone know it, about receptions where the tension was so high that people celebrated when the celebration was over.

She knew that any or all of these things could happen. She and her former husband hardly had spoken for years, and he had little to do with their daughter, financially or emotionally.

Nevertheless, the young woman asked her father to walk down the aisle. He agreed and surprised them by offering financial help. Then when he arrived, he asked his former wife, "Would you mind if I reply 'her mother and I do' when the minister asks who gives her away?"

The woman, touched by his eagerness to include her, cried for the first of many times that day.

She cried when her daughter walked down the aisle in an old-fashioned dress of lace, when her daughter's grandfather danced with her, and when her son rose to toast his sister and tell how proud he felt when she walked down the aisle. "I want my little sister and everyone here to know I love her," he said.

None of the bitterness between former relatives or new spouses and boyfriends emerged as she had been warned.

"My parents and other relatives went out of their way to make my ex-husband and his wife and the bridegroom's mother feel extremely welcomed," the woman said. "Everyone made sure my daughter was the center of attention, and nothing was going to spoil that. It was an undiscussed, known feeling."

She was especially touched by her former husband's caring behavior toward the children and her. At the rehearsal dinner, "It was as though he were reaching out to me and history, talking about times when the kids were little," she said.

She did not know what had changed him, she said, but she thought it might have been an incident a few months before when he learned that his son, attending a college near where his father lived, had gotten into some trouble. It was a problem the father could have averted.

When the father asked his former wife, "Why didn't you call me?" she replied: "Because you would have bawled him out instead of asking to help."

The mother believes that incident made her former husband begin to think about what kind of a father he wanted to be and how lucky he was to have good children.

After the wedding, he found his former wife in a back room putting some things away.

"I wanted to tell you goodbye," he said, putting his arm around her. "And I wanted to thank you."

Later she told a friend, "For a man who has had nothing kind to say about me for years, I could tell that what he said was genuine.

"And I had the feeling he wasn't thanking me just for that day, but for raising those kids and giving them the love they needed so they could show it to each other."

* * *

"He (or she) did it to me and I'm going to get even" are the verse and chorus of a song sung by a great many divorced people.

Consequently, they spend their time nurturing the song of resentment so carefully that they cannot overcome the hurt caused by the breakup and begin to grow.

One of the subtle ways in which women get even is by remaining helpless: They cannot take care of the car, they cannot make decisions about money, they cannot get minor repairs done on the house.

Instead they call their former husbands, crying or raging, "See what you've done to me. You've left me all by myself, and I can't survive. You have to do it for me."

Often the ex-husband does. He feels guilty about leaving a woman for whom he has done everything without someone to do those things for her now.

In some instances, you might argue that he deserves the guilt, and he certainly is obligated to keep picking up the pieces he promised at the altar to do for a lifetime. But the greatest harm these women are doing is not to their former husbands, but to themselves.

Because they are telling themselves that they cannot do things, they never learn that they can. Because they are hanging onto their former husbands for constant help, they are not really looking for a new love. Because they have not worked through their resentments and fears, they are not likely to enter into and maintain a healthy relationship.

One woman I talked to was still calling her former husband after three years of divorce. When she told me about it, she cried. He had left saying she had to change because he couldn't take her clinging behavior anymore.

Since then, she had been working hard at changing —going to classes, reading books and calling him every week or so to tell him how she was changing in hopes that he would come back—even though he was living with another woman and told her that he wished she would quit bothering him.

Change is fine. We all change. Unfortunately, this woman was not trying to change into something she wanted to be; she was trying to become something she thought her husband wanted, and it was making her shaky and miserable.

Although she had been legally divorced three years, she had not been emotionally divorced yet. She desperately was hanging on to some erroneous ideas: that she could not survive without him; that she could not be herself and be lovable; and that if she became another person, she could get her husband back.

Actually, her chances of surviving and being happy again were going to be greater the minute she divorced him from her heart and mind and became as independent of him as possible.

Many divorced women would tell her this: Knowing that you can take care of yourself—financially, physically and emotionally—feels much better than hanging on or getting even.

* * *

It's tug-of-war time again in the divorce arena. And the spoils of summer are the children.

Mom puts her teenage son on a plane to visit his father. A few weeks later, he tells her all the exciting things they are doing: hiking, hang gliding, shooting the river rapids.

Mom experiences mixed emotions. She is glad he is having a good time, glad the relationship with his dad is going well because it is good for a boy to feel close to his dad.

But there is a knot of fear in her stomach, too. A fear much stronger than the initial concern over his health and safety.

"What if he decides he wants to stay with his dad?" she wonders. "What if he figures it's a lot more exciting there than it is here, where Mom is always yelling at him about improving his grades and keeping his room picked up?"

She doesn't sleep well that night. She won't sleep well until he gets off the plane, hugs her and another summer's danger is past.

The same mother, however, admitted to creating a similar vacation atmosphere for her visiting daughter.

"I keep trying to tell her it isn't like this all the time," she said, as she planned more trips like those they had taken to Old Tucson and the Grand Canyon. "But what do you do when you only see them for a few weeks a year? You want to do something special for them."

This woman is not trying to talk her daughter into choosing to stay with her, but she fears her ex-husband is trying to influence her son into remaining with him.

And her fears might be justified. A lot of non-custodial parents use vacation times to sell their children on moving in with them. And many kids, torn between love for both their parents, are easily influenced by the partylike "courting" atmosphere the non-custodial mother or father sets up for their stay.

One family I know built a new bedroom on the house for the husband's daughter after she decided she wanted to stay with them after spending vacation there. The next year, she vacationed with her mother, called her father and said she was staying with her mother.

The man was upset, feeling his daughter had let him down—as had his son, for whom he had custody, but who had moved back and forth several times from mother to father during his childhood and teenage years.

A divorced woman who had custody of her two children sent her teenage daughter to visit the children's father out of state one year and the girl called and said she wanted to live with her dad. The woman was devastated but comforted herself by saying, "She'll be back. I predict she'll be calling by Christmas—just as soon as she has enough time to find out what her dad is really like."

Sure enough, she wanted to come home at Christmas. But the mother, wisely, made her stay through the school year.

"By then, you'll be certain you really want to come home," she said. "I don't want you bouncing back and forth between us."

The daughter came home to stay that summer, but a lot of other kids never seem to be able to make a permanent commitment to either parent.

One woman who had watched her ex-husband

agonize repeatedly over his children's decisions to stay with him, then to return to their mother, angrily said: "I can't forgive them for what they are doing to their father."

Her feelings are understandable, but the kids are not really to blame. They are torn between the natural need to be with and love both parents. And they are too often pawns in their parents' ongoing divorce war.

* * *

His stomach hurt every time he drove into the driveway of the house.

This used to be his house. He and his wife had bought it during the good times when his sons were babies and they were all still laughing and loving a lot.

He had put up the basketball hoop that still hovered over the driveway. He had built the flower box in front and the brick barbecue in back.

Now his key wouldn't let him in. The locks had been changed. His wife was no longer his and he was a visitor in his own driveway.

The driveway was usually the closest he got. The kids came running out to meet him and he and his ex-wife exchanged a few curt words through the car window about coming-home times.

It was just as well. Whenever they got into longer discussions about financial needs, the kids' emotional crises, or worse yet, the good and bad times of their marriage, the pain would return so strongly that it took a day or two for him to get his equilibrium back.

This was such an unnatural state: He in an apartment where his own children were bored visitors. He and they trying politely to deal with the awkwardness of it all. Gone was the easy familiarity of living together that naturally flowed into loving and teaching.

Some days, he didn't want to discipline them because he saw them so seldom, so he found himself overlooking the times that John talked back to him or Ken didn't pick up the toys he got out.

Other times he overreacted, trying to squeeze weeks or months of discipline into a few hours time—lecturing them on manners, on eating well, on doing their schoolwork even though he saw their eyes escape him into their own thoughts.

Or he insisted that they help him with household chores and minor repairs around the apartment for their "own good."

"You've got to know how to put a washer in a faucet, for Pete's sake," he'd say. Even though he knew that they'd much prefer to be seeing the zoo with their mother and stepfather as they'd done last weekend. Even though he knew they'd now be more reluctant to come next weekend.

The boys were getting older and it was difficult to find times to get together. He would call to see when they would come over or to ask how they were doing, only to find they were on their way to some school activity. They would promise to call back, but seldom did.

"It's not that they don't love you," said a friend he was dating. "Teenagers are like that—they're pre-occupied with their friends—parents are only incidental."

"I know," he responded. "But if I were living there, at least I'd be able to talk to them as they were coming and going."

The difficulty of getting together, the strained politeness when they did and the sadness of pulling into the driveway of a home that was no longer his made it easier for him not to call them, either. He drifted into new relationships where guilt, frustration and lost dreams weren't so painful.

Soon, he hardly saw his sons at all.

* * *

The young woman tried to be a good mother to her stepdaughter, but it wasn't easy.

When she and her husband married, the child was 2 years old, had not yet been toilet trained, refused to go to bed and regularly used swear words.

So when the child visited, the stepmother toilet trained her, tried to instill healthy eating and sleeping habits, worked at cleaning up her language and, most importantly, gave her loving attention and special gifts in the hope of developing the bond she felt should exist between mother and daughter. But on both sides, there was resentment.

The child resented this strange woman trying to replace her mother and coming between her and her father. The woman resented the child's rejection of her affection, her hold on her father and the way her husband's ex-wife would leave the child with them at a moment's notice.

"I just don't think she should be able to call up here and drop Meredith on us anytime she feels like it," the stepmother said as she exploded in anger one Friday because the child's visit would force them to cancel a weekend trip.

Her husband returned her anger.

"She's my daughter, and I don't get to see her often enough as it is," he said. "You just don't like having her."

The child, even at 3 years of age, knew how to manipulate her father and anger her stepmother.

"You're not my mommy," she would say when asked to do something. And she would run to her father for comfort.

When the woman and her husband would cuddle on the couch to watch television, the little girl would climb between them, put her arms around her father's neck and say, "My daddy."

Her father, uneasy about not being a full-time father, enjoyed this affirmation of affection, and the child stayed between them.

His wife, realizing that she was dealing with a small girl as if she was the other woman, decided to get some help. She began to read books on stepparenting and to talk to people in similar situations.

A friend helped her adjust to the fact that no matter what she did, the stepdaughter would never love her as much as she loved her father or mother.

"She already has a mother," the friend said. "Think about how much you love your mother. How would you feel if someone told you that you had to love another woman as much? You can be her good friend, like a favorite aunt."

The woman also began to understand that most little girls want to be Daddy's girl and that the situation was worsened by her overreaction.

"Yes," she started to say, with a smile, whenever the child claimed him as "My daddy."

"He is your daddy. And he's my husband. Isn't it nice that we both love him and he loves both of us?"

As she tried harder to see things from the child's viewpoint, to keep a sense of humor and not to get into competition with the little girl, she regained control of the situation. The child became more manageable and the affection between the two began to grow.

With the tension eased, her husband felt less compelled to defend his daughter and listened more receptively when she discussed problems with him.

"It's certainly not perfect, but it's better," she told a

friend. "I still get mad inside about things, but sometimes, it's nice, too, like the other night we had dinner out and we had a good time, just like a real family."

Chapter 4

Oh, you kids!

Watching mothers push strollers and chase toddlers through a shopping center, I thought that if I were starting parenthood again, I would make this pledge to my newborn:

My child, I have decided to bring you into my life because I believe helping a small human being become a creative, loving adult is the greatest gift I can give to the world and to myself.

I expect raising you to be rewarding, even joyous at times but not easy, because any time you take another person into your life, you get the conflicts along with the blessings. And anything worth doing takes effort.

I promise to love you, to give you good food, clean clothing and a warm place to curl up when you need sleep or comfort; I promise to give you the shelter of my arms.

I promise to recognize that you are a special person—not like any other—not like me or like my aunt or any person I think you might be or should be like.

I promise to encourage you in the way you need to go or want to go even if I would like you to do something else.

I promise to praise you more often than I scold and to know you are a worthwhile person even when you're going through a bad phase like the "terrible twos" or the tumultuous teens.

I promise to understand that you are not perfect and never will be, that you are human—as am I. That you will make mistakes, have bad moods, bad habits, character flaws, and the most I can do is to help you learn to control and overcome them.

I promise to be there when you need me but also to encourage you to try things by yourself and discover your own strengths and to help you learn to say no to those things that are bad for you and go fearlessly after those that are good.

I'll try to teach you to think more often and more deeply, to watch perceptively and question easy answers and to help you become so sure of your own worth that you will not need to follow the lead of others to feel important.

I promise to listen and not jump in with lectures before you've said what you want to say. And I promise to be aware of your needs at those times when you want my help but don't ask.

I promise to have a sense of humor and not overreact when you try things I think are silly, to not take us or life so seriously that we can't be kids together occasionally and laugh together often.

I will try to put more enjoyment than worry into our relationship—to relax and understand that when you have a stomach ache it doesn't necessarily mean you are dying of a dread disease, and when you snitch your sister's drink it isn't a sure sign you are growing up into a selfish adult.

I promise to raise you to leave me—to encourage you to grow stronger and stronger so that you will feel capable of going first to spend the night at a friend's house and later to spend your life in your own house.

I promise not to blame you for changing, to recognize that each day, each year of your life will bring changes because life is a process of change.

And I know if I do all these things, chances are good that you will be a strong, wise, self-confident and caring adult. And you will be my friend.

* * *

"Don't get your hopes up" is one of those insidious destructive phrases loving parents use with their children for "their own good."

A man told me he has been fighting that admonition all his life. He knows his mother told him not to get his hopes up because she didn't want him to be disappointed. She had seen too many of her own hopes fade into the reality of life as she tried to raise a family in the Depression.

But, now in his 40s, he still is trying to overcome the legacy of doubt she gave him. Whenever he dares to dream of success, her warning comes back to haunt him and he is afraid to try because he might fail.

Parents do children no favors when they try to protect them from disappointment by instilling resignation or fear. For one thing, what is so frightening about disappointment? Most of us meet it and live through it a good many times in our lives. Being disappointed is certainly not as bad as being afraid to try.

"But you really want to keep your kids from being unrealistic," one woman said as we discussed this. "There are some things it's just not likely they can do."

That is possible, but I wonder how many kids who dreamed of making the Olympics never tried because their parents said not to get their hopes up. And how many are winning gold medals because their parents said they could?

We can encourage our kids to dream big and then point out the realistic steps—such as education or training—they need to take to get there. If disappointment comes, then we can encourage them to pick themselves up and dream again.

A woman once told me that her daughter had really wanted to be a journalist, but she told her jobs were hard to get and talked her into studying nursing instead.

"Oh, no don't do that," I said. "If she really wants a newspaper job and she's good, there'll be one for her."

Telling kids not to get their hopes up is basically telling them you don't believe in their ability to make good things happen in their lives. You don't expect much from them, so they don't expect much from themselves.

Psychology Today magazine recently reported another study supporting what it termed "one of the best established principles in psychology, the self-fulfilling prophecy." When teachers in a Jerusalem high school expected children to do well, they did. When they expected less, the children did less well.

"Students in classrooms, workers in shops, patients in therapy, rats in mazes all do better when the person in charge expects them to do well," the magazine stated.

Another article in the same issue discussed Olympic competitors' new respect for psychological training.

"At this level of competition, the difference between two athletes is 20 percent physical and 80 percent mental," clinical psychologist Michael Mahoney said.

In other words, no matter how good you are, if you

don't think you can win, you won't. If you don't get your hopes up, you will lose.

* * *

A young mother the other day tried to get her daughter to stop sucking her thumb by demanding, "What will people think?"

That started me thinking: How many times do we say that to our sons and daughters and then later wonder why they go along with the crowd? We're programming them to be followers when we tell them to worry about what other people will say.

We reinforce that attitude if we respond, when they want to do something differently, "You can't. Nobody does it that way."

We certainly should teach them to get rid of obnoxious habits, but I think we shouldn't make other people's approval so vital. Whenever we can, we should encourage them to do things differently; emphasize that there is value in being your own person, being creative.

Then, perhaps, our children will say to peers who pressure them to take drugs: "I don't care; I just don't want to do that."

* * *

The 3-year-old boy played about the living room as several of us visited his mother.

Occasionally, he would show one of his toy trucks to one person or another or attempt to climb up on a visitor's lap. His mother would say, "Johnny, go play with the cars. We want to talk."

Then she would tell us how "bad" Johnny was.

"I don't know what I'm going to do about him. Chris is so much better-behaved," she said, referring to the boy's 1-year-old brother. "He started sleeping through right away, and he doesn't demand attention all the time like Johnny does."

I looked at Johnny as he ran his truck along the arm of the couch. It bothered me that his mother could not see Johnny's good qualities, his sweet smile, his intelligence and his command of language, which made him seem older than he was.

As the guests started to leave, Johnny went to one of the women and, of his own accord, said, "Thank you, Mindy, for bringing me the truck."

Mindy reached down and hugged him.

"Oh, Johnny, you're such a good boy," she said.

Johnny looked up at her, his eyes round and solemn.

"No, I'm a bad boy," he said.

As we walked to our cars, Mindy and I talked about Johnny. As a teenager, would he try to live up to the image his mother had given him of himself? And would she then wonder why he was being a "bad boy"? Or would she say, "He never has been any good."

I've found that this incident is not a rare one.

A woman recently took her two daughters, ages 3 and 5, to a company picnic.

All afternoon, the mother kept urging the younger girl to "show them how you dance, Marti" and commenting on how sweet and talented she was.

"I don't know what happened to Genni," she said at one point, putting her arm around the older girl. "She seemed to be left behind the door when beauty and talent were handed out."

The mother's protective arm didn't erase the tense look on the child's face.

Sometimes hurt is inflicted in the guise of teasing. A muscular neighbor has been worried for years about his tall, thin son.

"Hey, look at old beanpole here," he said to friends one day, clapping a hand on his son's shoulder. "With that physique and those ears, we could put him in the garden to scare away the birds."

Pain tightened the boy's face. The father didn't see it, but a friend of mine did. We talked about it later.

"Well, he shouldn't let it bother him," my friend said. "His father was just teasing. He shouldn't be so sensitive."

Fortunately, some children are blessed with parents who use the power of words positively. One woman I know was called Miss Sunshine by her parents from the time she was an infant. I am certain that is why she has such a sunny, sweet personality at age 19.

The world and the people in it form the mirror in which we try to find an image of the kind of person we are. Words have immense power because people use them to reflect images of ourselves back to us.

It is important that we give Johnny—and the other people in our lives—a picture of himself as valuable. Then when he responds to life, he will do it in keeping with the self-image we have given him.

"I can do wonderful things," he will say enthusiastically. "I'm a good boy."

* * *

A 4-year-old boy ran ahead of the family, barely missing a potted plant in the restaurant foyer.

"Get back here, Roger," said the father, dragging him to where his 7-year-old sister and mother waited. The mother held the hand of a 2-year-old girl whose finger was in her mouth.

"Now I expect all of you to behave," said the father. "This is supposed to be a treat, so don't ruin it."

The woman's face was full of pleasure as she recalled a portion of her childhood.

"Dad used to take us places by ourselves, one at a time, and those were the really good times because we didn't have to share him," she said. "I liked it best when he'd come in and wake me up early on Sunday morning and whisper, 'C'mon, let's just you and me go fishin'."

They had barely been seated when the 4-year-old knocked over a glass of water. His big sister glared at him, her face a mirror of her father's anger. "See what you did," she said. The boy, chastened, scooted down in his seat, his chin on his chest. His father signaled a waiter and his mother, too frantic to comfort the child, tried to mop up the mess with a napkin.

His mother and father couldn't afford fancy outings, but he didn't mind, said the successful businessman. He loved the days when the whole family went mushroom picking.

They'd carry picnic lunches that they'd eat beneath the northern Michigan trees when they tired of finding mushrooms. The kids would play, the adults would talk and sometimes an adult would play with them.

The 2-year-old kept standing up in her chair to jabber at older diners. Her father kept pushing her down as he corrected the children's table manners.

"Karen, for Pete's sake, use your knife and fork. Roger, where's your napkin?" Then to his wife: "I'm embarrassed to be seen with these kids. You'd think they grew up in a barn."

Roger suddenly knocked over his milk.

"That does it!" said the father. "If we ever get

through this, we are never going to go out to eat again."

The woman sipped a cup of coffee in her farm home and said she'd been worrying because they couldn't afford building materials to finish the girls' rooms.

"I wanted them to have memories of a nice room of their own," she said. "And now they're teenagers and are going to be grown before we get the rooms done."

One of her daughters entered the living room and placed a hand on her mother's shoulder.

"Are we going to get up tomorrow and check the plants?" she said. "It's Saturday."

"Sure honey," said the mother.

"Good," said the girl, who then left.

"We all get up on Saturday morning early," explained the mother, "and get cups of coffee and cocoa and then we go all around our property and check the trees and flowerbeds. It's so much fun, finding new buds and sprouts. The kids love it and so do my husband and I. It's a really special time together."

* * *

The first thing we have to do if we want to communicate wisely with our children about sex is to get over the feeling that sex is someone's dirty secret. It's difficult because most of us were raised to believe sex was something you didn't talk about, except in whispers.

Actually sex is as natural as eating and breathing. Human beings do it; animals do it. What makes sex special, however, are two things: Sex is an act of creation. Sex in its highest form is also an act of love.

Breathing and eating maintain life; sex creates and

enhances it. Therefore sex should be talked about as both natural and special, not as shameful and wrong.

Once we can convince ourselves of that, we are halfway home because when our children ask the questions, we'll be comfortable with the answers. And they'll be comfortable asking the questions.

As any parent knows, the kids start asking early.

"My son asked the final question at 5," one mother told me. "He was a child who would never take half an answer for anything. He kept at you until he had the whole story."

One night as she tucked him into bed, he pressured her, "But HOW does God plant the seed in the mommy."

"My husband and I had decided to let God take all the credit for the time being," said the mother. "But since my son wasn't satisfied, I excused myself, telling him I'd forgotten to do something in the kitchen."

In the kitchen, she described the situation in low tones to her husband, who responded, "Tell him he can know when he's older."

She returned to her son's bedside and said, coolly, "Now what were we talking about?" He had not forgotten. "I want to know how God plants the seed," he said.

"I'll tell you when you're older," the mother said.

"Oh, Mama," he said, exasperation in his voice. "Go back in and ask Daddy if I can know now."

So she told him. And it was never the worry she had thought it would be. He grew up with healthy attitudes about sex.

I found the same true with my son and daughter. We talked about sex from preschool and thereafter, whenever they brought the subject up or whenever I thought they needed information.

I bought them books on sexual growth and loving

that suited their ages, and later, when indiscriminate sex became the vogue in movies and television, we talked a lot about how even something as special as sex can be misused and hurtful. Love and commitment should be its natural companions.

The talking was not always easy. I had a lot of 1950s hang-ups, and there were many times I had to swallow hard and assuage my own uneasiness before I could deal naturally with their questions.

A friend of mine found that learning to be open and easy about the subject had its rewards.

When her daughter was 13, the girl went to camp, where one of her friends was caught in bed with a boy. Talking about it later, my friend asked her daughter what she thought.

"Well, I think it is all right if she loves him," the girl said.

That was one of the times my friend swallowed hard. She swallowed fear and she swallowed anger. But she asked calmly, "How many times do you think she might be in love before she finally gets married?"

Her daughter responded with instant dismay. "Oh," she said, "and what if she did it with all of them!"

* * *

A place of our own—that's what we wanted when we built the hide-out across the field, amid the mesquite trees on the other side of the ditch bank.

It seems most of us as kids longed for a private place to think private thoughts, to say private things, with no adult eyes and ears to censor or stop us. It's not that we were going to say or do anything bad, it's just that we wanted one place controlled by us in a world controlled by adults.

Perhaps this need is stronger in a child growing up with lots of other children; I don't know. But my brothers and sisters and I never had a room to ourselves, and often we shared beds. Perhaps a child who has a room all his own doesn't need to build a hide-out.

All I know is that I remember liking to build places in which to hide when I was very young. It began with blankets draped over chairs and tables in the living room. It was dark and cozy, and the tile floor was cool to curl up on with my doll and dream, or to sit on and talk secrets with a best friend.

As we grew older, my brothers and sisters and I got more adventurous. Across our field, across the neighbor's field and on the other side of the ditch, next to a dirt road, was a thick grove of mesquite trees.

Exploring those trees one day, we noticed that the hanging branches created at least five natural rooms. And in one corner of the "living room" was the piece de resistance—a bush that had grown in such a way as to form a little bower of green.

Thus began one of those projects that amaze parents. Children who balked at taking out garbage or picking up their rooms spent hours on hot summer days cutting stickery tree branches, hauling out dead wood and trash, sweeping dirt floors and loving every moment of it.

But it was ours. Our house. No adult ever set foot in it. We ran it our way.

To make it even more private, we climbed tamarisk trees nearby and cut off large bushy branches to weave into the barbed wire fence separating the mesquite trees from the road.

For days and days we worked until we had a shady, private nest with smooth dirt floors, rooms furnished with odds and ends of wood and a place to sit for private talks in the living room bower. We were certain that only the frogs and bugs that sang in the nearby ditch, over which we had built a shaky board bridge, knew our secret place.

But one afternoon, after chores at home, we came to play and everything had been torn down. It was not the storm the night before, we knew, because the hide-out had survived worse storms.

No, this was deliberate destruction. The wooden furniture we had nailed together had been torn apart and scattered, the tamarisk branches had been pulled out of the fence and thrown about.

It had to be the work of the Bad Boys—a group of older boys on the next block whose purpose in life, it seemed, was to make life miserable for little kids.

We cried, got angry and built the hide-out again. Again the Bad Boys tore it down. Again, we built it, again the Bad Boys tore it down.

Finally, we didn't rebuild it. The summer was almost over anyway, and school would start. There would be no more time for hide-outs. The Bad Boys won.

Or did they? I drive by the old mesquite grove now, and I remember with pleasure how it felt when a bunch of us kids had a place of our own for a few weeks one summer. The Bad Boys can't destroy memories.

* * *

She had been worried, she said, about her kids being overscheduled, and had suggested her 9-year-old daughter drop ballet lessons.

We talked, then, about kids and mothers we knew who spend every evening and weekend days racing from lessons to classes to meetings. About dinners eaten in the car on the way to piano lessons; spelling lessons in the car on the way to Scout meetings, and clothing changed in the car on the way to gymnastics lessons.

"I really felt that my son and daughter and I had no time to talk anymore," she said. "I wanted them to have some time to just think some thoughts of their own, to dream a little, to just play with the dog."

We talked about our own childhoods and unscheduled time. She and her friends liked to put on puppet shows. They would scour the alleys for old boxes, scrounge up costumes from closets and neighbors.

"We just had a lot of time, so we could make up things," she said.

So did my brothers and sisters and I. Out of spare time came neighborhood plays, poems written just for the fun of it, parades, carnivals, hide-outs and games.

The mother and I talked about the hours we both had spent with other kids, playing games of "Mother, May I?" and hide-and-seek. About gathering a mixture of kids—all sexes, ages and abilities—to play baseball. Then working out our own games, our own rules, our own problems.

"You just don't see kids doing that anymore," she said. "It's sad. We had such a good time. Now the games are so structured, and the adults run them."

Besides chores and homework, one of the structured things we had to do in our family was take piano lessons. My mother believed a child wasn't properly raised without knowing how to play the piano.

So when my son was 8, I wanted him to take piano lessons. He balked. Using reasoning beyond his years, he said, "Mama, I'm doing a lot already. I'm writing books; I'm painting pictures; I'm in the play at school. Why does a boy need to do anything else?"

He was right. I didn't require him to take the lessons just because it was a family requirement for the perfect upbringing.

I decided instead that the perfect upbringing was one that produced an active, enthusiastic child, busy doing many things, creating a lot of things—many of them in his spare time.

I believe we need to rethink "spare" time. Spare is defined by Webster's as "not used" or "over and above what is needed." In other words, superfluous.

I maintain that "spare" time is probably the most important time a child has. Far from not being used, spare time leads to true creativity, which is distinct from the creativity of craft classes, where the theme and materials are provided by an adult.

Those are good, of course. However, unstructured time is when children learn the creativity of producing something from nothing but their own minds: the puppet shows, the hide-outs, the poetry, the pictures, the thoughts about where the bug is crawling to or why the wind makes a sound in the trees.

I am grateful for those times in my life. Because of them, I know that my mind can create what I need when I need it—whether it is making decorations from something around the house for an impromptu party or coming up with an idea for a column.

As the mother said, it's vital that we make sure our children have time to talk, dream, pet the dog. And, especially, to think their own thoughts. Something wonderful, something all their own, can come of it.

* * *

Two recent studies support my belief that the dedication of a parent is the most important factor in successfully raising children.

Whether you stay at home with the kids full time or divide your time between home and a career, your child will most likely do well if he knows by your actions and attitude that you believe he is a special, lovable person.

In a recent survey by the National Association of Social Workers, 60 percent of 307 single mothers in 12 states and the District of Columbia said they believe their families are stronger than two-parent families. Twenty-five percent said they are just as strong.

The single mothers said relatives and friends help. They also said there is more harmony (no divided leadership between the parents), and that their kids develop independence and determination.

A separate study examined 573 children of working mothers in 38 states. Researchers at Kent State University in Ohio found that children of working mothers have higher IQs, get better grades and earn higher ratings from their teachers than do those with stay-at-home mothers.

Before stay-at-home mothers get upset, I suggest they wait a few weeks and there will probably be a survey published—as in the past—saying kids fare best with a mother who is home all the time.

From what I've experienced, I would say all the surveys are right.

I was reared by a stay-at-home mother and thought it was the best way to grow up. But then I was a working single mother and, despite worries about child care and lack of time, my children and I "grew up together" to be best friends.

I have several friends who have wonderful adult children they raised all by themselves. I also have friends who stayed at home and raised wonderful adult children.

I see some common factors in all these successful parents:

• They considered their children to be thoroughly worthwhile humans. The kids might do things they needed disciplining for, but they were never "bad" kids.

• The parents were there for them, either reachable by phone or ready to talk when they got home. The parents made the kids' activities a priority by attending ball games and talent shows.

• The kids and parents talked a lot, and about almost everything. Few topics were off limits. The kids felt safe about bringing up their worries, their offbeat ideas.

• The parents listened a lot and listened closely, watching for things the kids weren't saying. They also were aware of changes in their children's behavior, so they knew when to initiate a long talk.

• The parents endured the tough times, setting rules and saying no when it was necessary.

• The children's friends were welcome in their homes. Often, the friends talked to these open-minded adults about things they couldn't discuss with their own parents.

• The parents emphasized the importance of doing well in school.

• Chores were important because the kids knew their help was needed to keep the family functioning properly.

The child's importance to the family was emphasized in every way. The kids sometimes had to give up their own activities to be there to applaud a brother or sister when they were performing in a play. They were expected to plan and join family celebrations.

While their own activities were supported, they also knew they spent Christmas with family and were there to celebrate other family members' birthdays.

• The kids and parents had fun together. They took

trips, played miniature golf or tag in the park.

The sense of commitment and of enjoying each other was far more important in these successful families than whether or not a parent was single or worked outside the home.

* * *

The 15-year-old boy and his mother would be seeing each other for the first time in three years. The mother was both excited and worried. She knew he would be almost a man now, that he had gone through a lot since she saw him last. It would be like seeing a stranger.

They had a lot of talking to do. About his running away from his father's home. About why he was now in a special camp for abused children. About his coming to live with her, eventually. About their relationship.

She had given custody of him to his father when the boy was 4 years old because the boy had serious medical problems. The father could provide the home care and the constant trips to the doctor he needed.

But she and the boy spent each weekend together until he was 12, when the father and stepmother moved across the country, taking him with them.

For the first years he was gone, the mother and the boy were in constant contact by mail. Then, suddenly, he stopped responding to her letters. Months passed. She kept writing, asking why he wasn't answering. She comforted herself, thinking he was a typical teenager, too busy to remember to answer.

Then she got a call from a social worker telling her he had run away from home and that he had been physically and emotionally abused by his father and stepmother.

The mother wanted to get him immediately, but the social worker said it would be better if he first spent a year at a wilderness camp that had remarkable success with rehabilitating abused children.

So the mother and son wrote, talked on the phone and made plans for her first visit to the camp four months after he was placed there.

When she arrived, she discovered her fears about their meeting were unfounded. Her son was overjoyed to see her. For the first three days of her four-day visit, he was charming.

They sat in his shelter or on logs under the night sky and talked about her life, why she and his dad divorced, why his father had custody instead of her, why his stepmother and his father did the things they did.

He read to her from his school journal and asked her what to do about some of the problems he was having with the other kids. He also confessed his fears that his behavior and things other people said about him would make her stop loving him.

"No matter what anybody tells me or what you do, I am still going to love you, and I am still going to want you to come live with me," she said.

The evening before she was supposed to leave, a counselor warned, "Tomorrow, he's going to really test you and see if you're going to be there for him even if he's bad. You may as well get ready, because he's going to be 180 degrees different than he's been these last three days."

Sure enough, most of the next day her son ignored her. When she finally persuaded him to talk to her, he said he didn't consider her to be his mother, that he didn't want her to write to him or call him or send him anything, that he just wanted her to leave him alone.

"Tough luck," she responded, fighting back the hurt. "I am your mother. I'm going to be your mother until the day you die. I am going to write to you and send you things, and what you do with them is your choice. But you are stuck with me, and that is that."

His only response was that he wanted to go eat, and he left. As the mother got ready to leave, the counselor said she wished the boy had been able to say goodbye in a positive way, because it was going to take him weeks to work it out once he realized what he had done.

The mother was putting her luggage in the car when the counselor said, "Well, look at this!"

The mother turned around. Racing toward her down the trail was a tall, lanky boy, tears streaming down his face. A minute later, he was in his mother's arms."

* * *

He had been reading all these magazine articles about supermoms, he said, but what about superdads?

The articles point out how tough the modern woman's life is as she juggles two jobs—home and career. And how she feels she has to be super at both.

He sympathized, he said. He knew just what they were talking about.

He was trying to juggle two careers, too. His wife works nights so he leaves a hectic day as a manager to pick up his toddlers from a babysitter.

"They're both clamoring for my attention," he said. "But by the time I get them dinner, get them ready for bed and get the housework done, I don't have as much time for them as I wish I did."

He has a clear case of what used to be exclusively a woman's malady; the working mother's guilt.

If he works late, he feels guilty because it cuts into

his time with the kids. If he leaves the office before the work is done, he feels guilty about not finishing it.

In the past, a father had one job—to provide financial support for the family. It was understood that the wife would raise the children and that Dad didn't have to be there a lot to be a good father.

Working late at the office meant, in most instances, that he was trying to advance his career so he could pay for his daughter's new bike, his son's tennis lessons and later their college education. Now he's not only expected to provide the money for those things, but he's got to spend a quantity of quality time with his children as well.

Much has been written about the emptiness of the time when a father wakes up in the middle of his lush office and lucrative career to find that he doesn't know his children. When he tries to reach out to them, they rebuff him, saying, "Where were you when I needed to talk, when I needed you?"

The enlightened, modern father wants to avoid this. He wants more contact with his children, beginning in the delivery room. He gives them their night feedings and makes their school lunches; he bathes, dresses and comforts them.

Instead of just "fathering" his children by giving them life and daily bread, he's also "mothering" them by giving them love and daily care.

But like a supermom, he's paying a price. He has eaten of the apple: He knows now the pleasure of closeness with his children and he doesn't want to give that up. At the same time, he wants to excel at his job, be promoted and make money so he can buy better things for himself and his family—as his father did. He's straddling the fence bvetween two eras, and it isn't comfortable.

I'd like to tell him: Hang in there, Dad. Do the best

you can and don't waste your already taxed energy on guilt. Your kids will survive if you're late to get them once in a while. Your job will survive if you leave it early once in a while.

Despite your perch on the fence, I know you realize you've made the right choice and that the answer is not to go back to being an always-at-work father whose kids don't know the joys of his embrace or what it's like to hear his bedtime stories—whose children grow away from him long before they grow up.

* * *

I was his first child. There were seven after me.

He held me and rocked me and sang to me and persuaded me to walk to him. He taught me to talk, which, when I was a teenager, I'm sure he regretted.

He built swings and sand piles and toys and furniture and our house. He sawed and painted late into the night and still got up early to awaken us with a whistled duet with the mockingbirds.

He planted trees, vegetables and flowers and irrigated them at 2 in the morning, standing in the water in black rubber boots, looking at the moon reflected in the ditch in front of him.

He played the piano by ear, as well as the harmonica, and when he played, his whole body moved with the rhythm. When he abdicated the piano bench so my mother could play for family sings, he rocked and sang the hymn **Love Lifted Me** *in a rich baritone.*

He read almost constantly and could never understand why his kids didn't enjoy reading the encyclopedia just for the fun of it, as he did.

He pretended he thought too much was made of Christmas and other holidays at our house. But he painted old bikes to make them new, built doll furniture and burst through the door on a December evening, excited about the bargain he got on a special Christmas tree.

He seldom liked to go to other people's houses for parties or dinner, but he loved to have people come to his—especially his own grown children with their children, especially on Thanksgiving and Christmas and Mother's Day and any time the weather called for a family volleyball game.

He sold, at different times, real estate, novelty items and furniture he built himself. He delivered bread and built airplane wings and won cash awards for methods he invented that made wing-building easier.

He wrote songs about his kids and later his grandchildren and composed poems to his wife in which he expressed feelings he found difficult to say. And she cried.

He raised pigs and horses, milked his cow and goats, and plowed fields to grow feed for them. His kids rode behind him on the tractor.

He brought home bargains like old chairs or pieces of pipe or unused bedsprings from auctions and secondhand stores, which he stored for days or years and eventually sold at a profit. In between the buying and selling, his kids had the use of them for playhouses and forts and fairy-tale games.

He told stories of how his father had died when he was 9, and he had become the "father" to a family of nine children during the Depression. He told of how his clothes were too small and the food was too little and his mother's face was drawn with worry.

He told of how he hitchhiked across the country to pick fruit in California and ended up in Arizona, where he remodeled a boarding-house and met my mother.

He seemed, when I was little, to always be strong and powerful. But as I grew older, I found the pain of *his childhood had left him vulnerable, and he could be hurt easily. I learned he felt and was deeply moved by more things than I ever knew.*

He taught us to work hard and to sing while we did it. He taught us to live well and to think while we did it. He respected intelligence, creativity and, above all, honor.

He taught us first about love and later about God. And somehow they and he seemed connected.

Thank you, Dad.

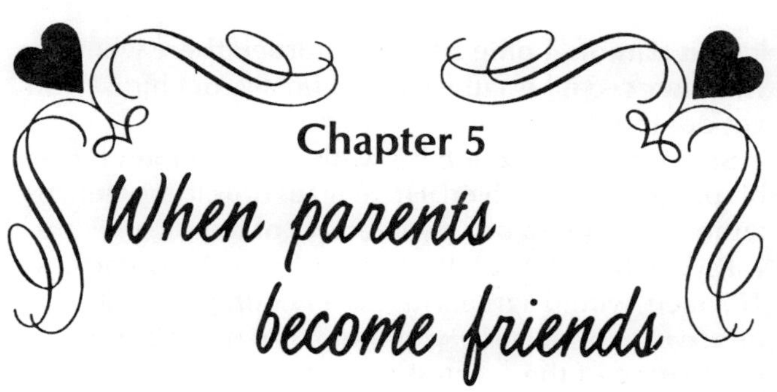

Chapter 5
When parents become friends

There was agony in the voice of the woman as she talked to her friend in the restaurant booth next to me.

"My daughter is pregnant again," she was saying. "She expects me to raise this one, too, but I told her I can't hack it. I'm tired of running after kids. But now she won't speak to me and just walks around the house looking like she hates me."

The woman had told her unmarried daughter to move out and take responsibility for her children and her life.

"She will probably never forgive me," the woman said. "And I keep thinking, 'What kind of a mother would kick her daughter and her grandchildren out?' But, darn it, she's got to grow up someday."

I thought of that woman this week after I read a magazine article about the increasing number of parents dealing with adult children returning home. And I thought of one mother of six who said she had taken all of her children back home for brief periods of time.

"There just seems to be a transition time, where they kind of move back and forth," she said philosophically.

However, not all kids see it as a temporary arrangement. A man I know said he probably wouldn't have left his parents' home after he returned there when he was divorced if his father hadn't finally told him: "You get out tomorrow."

So he left with no job but with a small stipend from his parents. He survived. He realizes now that when his father kicked him out it was an act of love.

Psychiatrist M. Scott Peck in the book, *The Road Less Traveled,* would agree. He calls encouraging independence in a loved one—whether it be friend, spouse or child—one of the greatest gifts of love.

The problem is in knowing when it is loving to provide a nest for a child and when you should insist he fly. A stay when an adult child is in desperate financial and emotional need is a loving thing to do. However, one family mentioned in the magazine article took their daughter back with no requirement that she contribute financially because she wanted to travel and have nice things and couldn't do that on her own.

That is not love. That is keeping the child from maturing. She won't learn the strength that comes from "toughing it out" and the self-confidence in knowing that she can do it herself.

Two years ago, a man I know made the rough decision to "kick his daughter out financially." He was regularly sending money to her because her husband was periodically out of work.

The daughter refused to get a job to help support them because she said, "My husband doesn't want me to. He says other people will think he can't support me."

The father, finally fed up that the husband's pride would keep him from having his wife work but not from taking money from his father-in-law, informed them that he was giving them no more money and not even $10 bills in letters.

The daughter was furious at first but later got a job and soon was telling everyone proudly how well she was doing at work and how good she had become at managing money.

"She has grown up so much," said the father. "Just because your children are adults in age, doesn't mean you've quit having to raise them. At some point, you've got to be an old meanie and tell them to make it on their own. It's the only way they learn they can."

* * *

The son greeted his father. They hadn't seen each other in several weeks.

"You're too skinny," the older man said. "You ought to be lifting weights. Get some meat on you. I'd be embarrassed to run around with my bones hanging out."

The son squirmed uncomfortably. This time he was going to tell his father how those comments made him feel.

"I wish you wouldn't talk that way, Dad," he said. "You're always putting me down, making me feel bad. That's why sometimes I don't want to see you."

The father laughed, shortly. Then he put his hands on his son's shoulders and looked him straight in the face.

"I'm telling you this for your own good," he said. "Besides, if you get hurt by something I say, it's your problem. What I say can't hurt you unless you let it."

The boy didn't say anything. He wished he hadn't come.

Later, he told a friend. "Ever since Dad got into all those consciousness-raising things, it's like he thinks he can say anything he wants to—that he has no responsibility for what kind of effect something he says has on someone else.

"It's like he thinks he can hurt someone and just walk away, saying it was their fault and not his. I don't care what he says. I think it's just cruel."

I think he is right. It's interesting how intelligent adults can take a legitimate idea and distort it. Many of the personal-growth books will tell you that if someone says something to hurt you, you don't have to accept that hurt. You can decide not to let it bother you.

That is good advice. After all, we control our own minds. We can decide not to accept someone else's criticism. We can just let it wash off and go on feeling good about ourselves.

But, as the boy knows, that isn't so easy, particularly when the criticism is coming from someone whose opinion you value, whose approval you seek—like your parent, spouse or friend. Surely his father, if he loves him, should be aware of that.

* * *

It's a war of love and, as long as parents and adult children fight for the other's approval, no one wins.

Children grow up looking to their parents for affirmation that they are worthwhile. "See what I did, Mama," they say, showing scrawled drawings of flowers and large-headed stick figures. And if Mom says it's wonderful, they feel good about themselves.

"I think the Dodgers will win because they have better pitchers," the preadolescent boy says to his father as they watch a Sunday baseball game. If his father replies, "You're right," the boy feels good about his judgment.

Then, if the boy asks his father who is going to win the pennant and the boy listens and believes, Dad feels good about himself.

When Mom explains to her daughter why she believes a particular political party is better for the country and the daughter agrees, the mother feels her daughter respects her wisdom.

Trouble begins when daughter and son start picking up new ideas from books, newspapers, television, teachers or friends. They sort through these ideas, re-examine some given them by their parents and develop ideas of their own.

They begin to argue with their parents' views on everything from living together before marriage to building nuclear power plants. They decide on careers, choose spouses and behave in ways their parents think they shouldn't.

"I can't believe you called up a man and asked him out," said a 62-year-old mother to her 35-year-old daughter recently.

"Why not?" said the daughter. "He was glad. We had a good time."

"He'll have no respect for you," said the mother. "Men don't respect forward women."

No matter how much they argued over the situation, neither could agree because they were from different social arenas.

But they argued anyway. The daughter wanted to win her mother's approval of her actions, as she had tried to win it all her life. The mother wanted to win her daughter's acquiescence to her greater wisdom, as the daughter had done as a child.

Each felt that if she didn't convince the other, she would not only lose the argument, she would lose value as a person—and thus lose the other's love.

And so they fight over big things, little things. They have difficulty accepting that there comes a time in our lives when we have to look at our parents and children as individuals separate from us, with their own ideas and ways of doing things.

We may not agree with them, but that doesn't make

what they think or do wrong. It just means they're different.

Our children are not replicas of us; they have a right to have minds of their own. Our parents have searched for and found a way of life with which they are comfortable; we should be glad they are happy in it, even if we wouldn't like to live that way.

It helps when we finally decide it's more important to have a loving relationship than to win our parents or children to our point of view. When we stop arguing and accept our differences, we discover that no fighting at all is the only way to win the war.

* * *

When I made an A on my math test, she was the first one I told.

When I got the part in the play, she was the first one I told.

And when a friend hurt my feelings, she was the first one I told.

When I decided to be a writer, she was the one I discussed it with. And she said she thought I'd be great.

When I had my first column published at 14, she was the one I bragged to. And she was the one who clipped it and sent it to all her friends.

When I had my first date, she was the one I told how nervous I was and how wonderful he was.

When I had my first child, she was the one I told how scared I was and how wonderful my daughter was. And she told me how she'd felt that way with her first daughter, too.

When I had problems with a husband, she was the first one I turned to. And she helped.

When I got a raise or a promotion, she was the first one I called because I knew she would enjoy it even more than I did.

When I decided to take a trip, she was the one I talked over my plans with. When I got back, she was the first one I wanted to tell about what happened.

When I wrote something good, she was the one I read it to. When I read something good, she was the one I gave a copy to.

When my children did something wonderful, she was the one I told because I knew she'd be prouder than I was.

When my children did something distressing, she was the one I told because I knew she wouldn't condemn them. She just helped me understand and solve the problem.

When I wallpapered my bathroom myself or planted a new tree in the yard, she was the first one I showed it to.

When I bought a new car, she rode in it and enjoyed it as much as I did.

When I gained an insight, she was the first one I called to share it with.

When I was feeling depressed, she was the first one I called to give me hope. And she always did.

When anything happened in my life—a friend hurt me, a letter touched me, a child surprised me, an experience distressed me, a book enlightened me, a song delighted me—she was the first one I told.

She was the first one I told everything, except how much she means to me.

Until now.

I love you, Mom.

Chapter 6

Goodbye, Grandma

My grandmother is dying. I am watching her die. Little by little, she goes.

Each time I see her, there is less of her—less weight on her suddenly frail frame. Less color in her face. Less life in her voice. Less laughter in her eyes.

She used to laugh a lot. She used to do a lot. She used to give a lot. Now it is all she can do to reach out her arms from the chair that swallows her and hug me.

Until the last few months, she gave my family flowers, raising them with tenderness around my parents' house so that they bloomed in profusion at our Easter get-togethers.

She insisted on caring for the trees, too, and the lawns and bushes because no one else could care for them as lovingly as she did. And on early summer mornings, she could be found harvesting radishes, asparagus and tomatoes she had raised to enrich her grandchildren's dinner table.

She gave us cards on birthdays, gifts at Christmas and comfort when life treated us badly. She gave us stories about her youth and words of wisdom about how to run the world today.

She knew what the City Council was doing, wasn't doing and should be doing. She had suggestions for Ronald Reagan and would have shaped up Menachem Begin if she had had a chance.

She seldom judged anyone. She simply saw them as only in need of enlightenment. She knew good people made mistakes. She forgave the mistake-makers of the world and loved those in her family with all her heart.

Now she cannot give as much. It takes all of her energy to hold onto the life she used to dwell in with gusto.

Each time I see her, I see two of her. I see her as she used to be and as she is now. Perhaps if I could not see her as she used to be, it would not hurt so much.

I see her in the little kitchen of her house, serving me sandwiches and freshly baked cookies. I see her spreading back the covers of her bed so I could snuggle in for the night and go to sleep listening to the radio and the gentle sounds of her breathing.

I remember the scents of her house. The swamp cooler sending a wet breeze across fresh straw pads. Cookies baking. Flowery-scented lotions and colognes and sachets.

I remember her in straw hat and overalls or colorfully striped apron planting flowers around the houses and trailers she called home during her life. I remember her showing me my aunt's scrapbooks and my mother's dolls and sitting together for hours on the carpet going through boxes of pictures of her as a golden-haired child, of her and my grandfather when they were first married, of my mother playing a clarinet in the school band.

I see her in church on Grandparents' Day, proud that I was there with her. I see her smiling as she gives me a potted shamrock for St. Patrick's Day, because she knows I love anything Irish as much as she does.

* * *

(I wrote this in June. Rhoda Mary Martins died Aug. 20, 1983. She is survived by all of us who love her.)

* * *

It has been six months since Grandma died. I feel peaceful and close to her.

It took time to achieve this peace. For months I felt sad, angry, guilty.

I didn't cry at Grandma's funeral or for a week afterward. I told myself and my friends that I didn't because I had cried almost every day for weeks before her death.

"I've done my grieving," I said.

A week after the funeral, I went to work and found I was unaccountably shaky and nervous. I could not write. I had not thought of a column idea in weeks, and I usually get three or four a day.

As I talked to co-workers about my grandmother, I realized I had been fooling myself. I had not finished grieving. I needed to cry for my loss again.

That night, I cried for a long time and felt better the next day.

But, irrationally, I was still angry at God for taking her. In the weeks before she died, I had been angry at him for not taking her and making her suffer.

During those weeks, I awoke one morning crying because I was afraid I wouldn't remember her the way she was when she was healthy. I was certain that she would stay in my mind as the sunken-faced woman she was in the hospital.

We also shared a love of dolls. She has her collection. I have mine. She was always rescuing discarded dolls and fixing them up. They sat, scrubbed and shining, next to stuffed animals under a small tree in the Christmas corner she fixed each year in her room.

She especially loved one of those dolls, partly because the dirt could not be cleaned off its nose, giving its cherubic face an impish look. I want that doll more than I can describe. I want to hold something tangible, something of her love, something of her that will not go away.

Oh, please don't go, Grandma. I don't want to say goodbye.

* * *

And I felt estranged from her in those last weeks because we could not communicate. I felt that I had failed her by not understanding what she was trying to say and by not knowing exactly what to do for her. I found myself wanting to die so we could be close again.

But for several months after she died, I still felt I had failed her, that we were not close. I was still angry at God. And I was preoccupied with death.

A friend pointed out that in a 15-minute conversation I had mentioned my fears about death in connection with a sister, a nephew and a friend. I had started and ended several sentences about what I wanted to do with the words "when I die."

Little things kept reminding me of Grandma. The magazines she ordered for me still came. The card store still carried grandmother cards. Everytime I took off a pair of hose with a run in them, I remembered I no longer had to save my old hose for her to wear when she worked in the garden.

At the end of December, I was looking at my plants on the ledge above my desk, and I realized that something in me wished the shamrock would die. That shocked me. It was given to me by my grandmother on St. Patrick's Day 1982. I can still see her sweet smile as she presented it to me. She was healthy and active then.

I think what bothered me was the plant wasn't healthy, and I didn't know what to do about it. It was symbolic of those long months we were waiting for Grandma to die.

The shamrock is still living, however, and I've finally realized I didn't fail Grandma. I've made peace with God, and my memories of my grandmother's face are of her when she was healthy and happy.

I have realized, too, that while Grandma gave me a lot in living, she also gave me some great gifts in dying. She brought my family closer together. I got to know and love some relatives I had not spent much time with before.

Also, as she lay dying, I began to evaluate my life and think about what I want it to have been when I die. And I knew that if I had won the Pulitzer Prize and had neglected those I loved, my life would have been a failure.

But, if I had not won any prize and, like Grandma, I had given the best I could to those I loved, I truly would be a success.

* * *

It's been almost three years since my grandmother died, and there still is hardly a day in which I don't think of her. Above my desk is the Easter card she sent me. On the shelf is the shamrock she gave me on St. Patrick's Day a year before she died. On shelves at home are a picture of her as a little girl and the dolls I now love as she loved them.

But all of these things bring no pain now. They make me smile as I remember her pleasure in her dolls and her delight in giving me the shamrock because a love for Irish people, legends and music was something special we shared.

Right after she died, I was devastated. A major part of my life had gone. She had taken the sympathetic ear I knew I could count on if I were having problems at work or at home. She had taken the loving smile that told me she thought I was special even if the rest of the world didn't.

She had taken the cookies she made for me at Christmas, the bouquets of flowers she picked for me when I came to visit, the loving cards sent on each holiday. Most of all, she had taken the promise of her presence each time I needed it.

Or so I thought at the time. Now I know differently.

If anything, my grandmother is more with me now than she ever was when she was alive. It's difficult to explain if you haven't experienced it, but I've talked with others who feel the same after losing someone they were very close to.

Grandma told me she felt that way when my grandfather died after 20 years of an especially happy marriage. "I feel as if he is still with me," she always said. It was one of the reasons she never married again.

I used to visit my grandmother or telephone her for comfort or counsel. Now I don't have to, her comfort and counsel are always with me.

I find myself measuring my behavior and my attitudes by her yardstick. Grandma stayed fully interested and involved in all aspects of life until she died; I will, too. She was not afraid of being alone or getting older; I don't have to be afraid, either.

Grandma was not a success as the world defines it. She had little money, no fame. But she gave and received love in great quantities. She showed me what real success as a human being is. So when I think I might not achieve the career goals I set for myself, I remember Grandma's lesson and regain my sense of priorities.

Even in day-to-day things, she helps me. For instance, one day my children and I were out together and a woman nearby made a cutting remark to them. Afterward, I nursed my anger at the woman for half an hour, thinking of things I wanted to say to her and unable to get myself back into the happy mood I had before she had intruded.

But then my grandmother came to mind, and I saw how she would have handled it. She just would have smiled and gently said, "Oh, well," meaning the woman couldn't help being the way she was and it wasn't a problem if we didn't make it one. Then she would have immediately forgotten it.

So I did the same. I let go of my anger and enjoyed the rest of the afternoon, just as Grandma would have.

When Grandma died and I sobbed in a friend's arms, he said, "Nobody will ever be able to take away from you all that your grandmother has given you."

He was right.

Chapter 7

Of aunts, sisters and other friends

Thirty-one years ago when I was 11 years old, my parents gave me the perfect gift: a living doll. I had wanted one ever since I read fairy tales about dolls who magically came alive. If I concentrated hard enough, I thought, perhaps I could make my doll come alive, too.

So in the morning or during nap time, I'd stare intently at my doll as she stood in her usual place on the dressing table, and I'd will her to live. Sometimes I even imagined I saw her move.

Then on my 11th birthday, my baby sister was born.

She was a tiny thing, barely 5 pounds. And she looked as unlike me as anyone could. I was blond and blue-eyed. She had dark skin, eyes and hair.

But she was mine. I bathed her, rocked her and dressed her just as I had done my dolls. And as she got older, it became a tradition for me to take her downtown for a day to see a movie, have lunch and spend our birthday gift money.

She was excited about that. She was excited about everything. She threw herself into life with a gusto that sometimes embarrassed her shyer sisters.

In the middle of a crowd, she would whoop, throw herself spread-eagled across a picnic table and gaze upward, loudly expressing her joy at the trees and sky. As a teenager, she was the most enthusiastic fan at football games, and when romantic scenes appeared on the television screen, she would hug herself and squeal.

She's older and a little more subdued now—but just a little. She still has a bubbling enthusiasm about her job, her family and her life. And when occasionally depression takes over, she blames no one but herself.

"I've got to get myself out of this," she says. And she does.

No one I know of is more committed to becoming a better person. She constantly works at being more understanding of unlikable people, more thoughtful of those around her.

She doesn't need to work so hard. No one is more thoughtful than she is or more enthusiastic about the good fortune of others.

When anyone is having a problem in the family, she's the first to try to help find a solution. When anyone is ill, she's the one who checks constantly to see if the person's doing better. If someone she knows needs something, she's likely to get it for him or her.

When I am feeling down, I talk with her and she says, "You're doing just fine. Don't let other people get to you." And I feel better.

When I tell her I'm setting some new goals for myself, she says, "This is exciting. I know you can do it." And suddenly I believe I can.

When I tell her about some success in my life, her reaction is to hug me and say, with tears in her eyes, "Oh, you really deserve it."

I don't know who decided 31 years ago that I deserved a sister like her. But I'm so glad I got her.

She is a living doll in the best sense of the words.

* * *

Once again, a friend and I were discussing what she wanted to do for a career.

"I know I want to make good money and be a success at something," she said. "But I don't know what I want."

She had been saying this for years. And for years I had been giving her advice on how to find out what she wanted. And each time I left her, she was certain of her goals and feeling good.

But in a few days, I would have to help her over the same rocky emotional territory. We had not solved a thing; I had just walked her through one of her lows.

As I get older, I'm learning that you can seldom solve problems for other people. All you can do is help them through a situation.

I cannot keep a beloved relative from getting old. I can just try to make it happier for him by talking with him, bringing books we can share, hugging him and letting him know how special he is to his family, even if he isn't able to remodel the house in one day like he used to.

I cannot make a young friend well and whole. His health and future are uncertain. All his friends can do is give him a telephone call, a job contact, a movie, their love.

And I cannot help a man who is trying to quit smoking. I can listen as he talks over and over again about cutting down and cutting out. I can share his enthusiasm that he is really going to do it this time, and I can encourage him when he is discouraged because he has failed again. But I cannot be his will-power.

All these apparently solutionless problems are difficult for me to handle. I'm a person who believes in solutions. My father raised me on the axiom, "You can do anything you really want to do," and for years,

I believed if there were a problem and I really wanted a solution, I could find it.

But as I've matured, I've discovered that even if I find a solution, some people don't want to hear it.

I learned this the hard way. I had always viewed myself as a loving, supportive friend. But recently when a friend who had been a homemaker for years was considering going to work and admitted being fearful, I encouraged her, telling her how great she would feel taking on the job market and taking home the paycheck. When we finished talking, she was calling for an interview.

Several weeks later, I saw her again. She had decided not to go to work, and she explained hesitantly that she had been afraid to tell me because she thought I'd be disappointed in her.

Another friend explained why.

"You always feel so certain someone should do something, you make people feel guilty for not doing what you think they should."

Ah, a rare chance to see myself as others saw me. Not a pleasant experience, that's for sure. But a learning one. And it's made me a better sister, daughter, mother and friend.

I know that when my children make career or romantic decisions I think are wrong, I'll just have to let them make their own mistakes and love them while they're doing it, even though I believe that if they had taken my advice, they could have avoided a lot of problems.

More importantly, I've learned I don't always know what is right for a friend or relative, no matter how well I know them or how clearly I think I see things. And they don't care, really, if I do because they don't really want me to solve their problems. They just want me to help them through another day.

* * *

We may forgive mate, child or parent for being imperfect, but we think friends should never let us down. They should always be there whenever we need them, no matter how great their need is to be somewhere else.

So if we're going to take a realistic look at friendship, we need to understand that friends can't always be there, emotionally or physically, when we want them to. Nor will most friendships be forever.

We move away from other people literally and figuratively. We change schools, jobs, towns. We change needs. Today we may need a friend to lean on, and she might need a friend to lean on her. As we become stronger and more self-sufficient, we may need a different kind of relationship.

But in a basically healthy friendship, there are certain things a friend does and does not do.

A friend does not remind you that you are getting fat so you shouldn't have dessert. She knows your struggles are your business and when you want help, you will ask.

She does not tell you she saw your ex-husband with a gorgeous brunette at the country club the other night. She pretends it never happened.

She remembers to return the books you loaned her and forgives you when you forget to return hers. She does the same with money.

She understands when you're too busy to talk on the telephone or to go to a movie and means it when she says, "We'll do it another time."

She sticks up for you when other people are putting you down; she also sticks up for you when you're putting yourself down.

She listens to you even when she doesn't want to—even when she's heard the same old song about the same old problems over and over again—because she knows it makes you feel better.

She enjoys the same things you enjoy. So when you see a movie together you enjoy it twice as much because she laughs when you do and she cries when you do. And she wants to spend hours afterward talking about what it meant—as you do.

She does not repeat the bad things she heard someone say about you. Instead, she repeats everything good she hears, embellishing it some to make you feel even better.

She doesn't forget you when she moves up in the business world but tries to bring you along, too.

She doesn't bring you down more than she lifts you up.

She tells you things she would never tell anyone else because she knows you will keep her secrets just as she does yours.

She isn't jealous of your other relationships; she knows you need different kinds of people in your life to fill different needs. And that includes other friends.

She doesn't hold a grudge when you let her down. She knows you are human and friendships are just like other relationships—the people involved make mistakes.

She also understands that, as in other relationships, friendship ebbs and flows. There can be jealousy, misunderstanding and discovery of things you don't like as well as things you do.

Sometimes you are as close as sisters and sometimes, like sisters, you don't enjoy each other much. But most of the time, you are both thankful for a relationship that allows you to be so completely and safely yourself.

* * *

An aunt is a family's gift to its children.

While you are growing up, an aunt surprises you with gifts on your birthday or graduation. Parents are supposed to give you gifts, and they often give you practical ones. But an aunt will send you something totally impractical. (If it's money, it's an impractical amount.)

An aunt sees you as being uniquely talented at singing or writing or making her laugh while your parents see you as uniquely talented at causing them problems. Your parents have to worry about bringing you up in the way they and the world think you should go. Your aunt doesn't.

If you misbehave, no one is going to look at her and, with a shake of the head, say, "Tsk, tsk, what a terrible aunt that child must have." So she can afford to enjoy you. She can laugh when you get a little too big for your britches, and let your parents worry about sending you to your room. She can let you have iced tea, even though it might stunt your growth.

When you get older, you begin to see your aunts as people with multifaceted personalities instead of just another tall—but especially nice—blurred image in the world of adulthood. You talk, share confidences, ideas. You become friends.

I'm lucky to have aunts who are friends: An aunt in West Virginia who sent me birthday gifts and boxes of her daughter's outgrown clothes and who wrote notes about how proud she was of me.

An aunt in Phoenix with whom I spent the night as a child, who baby-sat for my infant daughter when I went to work and who held me as I cried about my grandmother's illness.

An aunt in Hawaii, who wrote a poem about my antics as a toddler when 10 years' difference in our ages made all the difference. Later, she shared with me sun-drenched afternoons on the beach and long dinner conversations at restaurants when 10 years made no difference at all.

I don't know which is better—to have an aunt or to be one. If you are an aunt, you can have all the pleasures of grandparenting while you are still young enough to be one of the kids. You can give a niece lectures on life's goals from the soapbox of experience, but still swoon with her over Superman's smile in the movie theater.

And while kids see grandparents' attentions as part of their birthright, they don't expect things from an aunt. So anything you give them—a gift, a hug, a moment of understanding—is really appreciated.

"You make the kids feel special," my sister said once after I'd done something for one of my nieces.

"They make me feel special," I responded.

That feeling of being special is what aunts and nieces and nephews give each other. Because they are not obligated by birth as children and parents are, they can freely choose to love and care for each other.

An aunt is one of life's best things to have—and to be.

Chapter 8
The all-too-human race

Imagine a world in which you know what everyone else is thinking about you. Worse yet, imagine a world in which everyone knows what you are thinking.

It could blow your mind.

But when *Psychology Today* magazine asked readers the question: "If you were granted one supernatural power, what would it be?" most turned down the chance to be invisible, to fly or to move objects with their thoughts. They wanted to read other people's minds.

Most of them seemed motivated by paranoia, agreeing with the 18-year-old woman who said, "I want to know what people are thinking about me."

I am paranoid, too. That is why I never want to know what people are thinking about me. I prefer to believe they really mean those smiles and polite things they say about the way I look and write.

Besides, being able to read minds would take all the excitement out of living.

You would know what your child was really doing after school when he told you he helped the teacher. In fact, you would always know what your children were doing or thinking of doing, and anyone who has been a child or a parent knows that there are some things parents are better off not knowing.

Being able to read others' minds would take the romance out of life. You would discover that the come-hither look you are getting from the handsome guy in the restaurant has nothing to do with your new hairdo. He just thought of something that happened last night.

You would know what your husband really thinks when he tells you how much he likes that new dress you are so crazy about.

You would know what the people in the office think about the way you do your work, and you would be mad at everybody. Nobody ever thinks anybody else does what he should, and everybody always thinks he could do the job better—especially the boss' job.

Most of the people who said they would like to read other people's minds probably meant that they wanted the power all to themselves. But this is a free country. Once one person is given the power, it is only democratic to give it to everyone.

How awful that would be. In any open-minded world, you could not escape into your thoughts. It would be like living naked in a glasshouse. You would never know when someone might come by and see you.

You would suddenly be preoccupied with two things: avoiding the thoughts of others and controlling your thoughts. You would be afraid to have fantasies. You would be afraid to run into someone you disliked in the hall because he would sock you one.

Your kids would be yelling: "Mom, he's thinking at me." You would not know whom to vote into office because you would know the whole truth about every candidate. You would not marry anyone because you would know all his or her faults on the first date.

Of course, there always would be some people who would find a way to make money out of the situation. There would be a sudden surge of mind-control classes and a flood of books on "The Art of Thinking."

Some emotional good might come out of it. We might learn quickly that we could not please everyone so we would put our energies into being ourselves and quit worrying about what other people think.

But the art of conversation would be lost. We would not need to ask other people what they think, feel or believe. We would already know.

Personally, I do not want to think about a world in which everyone knows what everyone thinks. I would rather fly.

* * *

"I've begun to realize," said a friend, "that my husband doesn't really want my advice while he's going through this rough time. He just wants me to listen with understanding."

She's right. When we've got a problem, most of us don't want a lecture, we want a "listen."

When I told another friend of my worries about a nephew going through some rough times, he kept telling me not to let it get to me so much. The next day, a woman told me that when she told her husband about how upset she was after a minor accident, he said, "I don't know why you're letting it upset you. It's no big deal."

The woman and I discussed how we felt the men's reactions, while well-intended, made us feel worse.

They negated our feelings, said they weren't worth anything and that we were stupid for having them.

Shortly after her talk with her husband, the woman said, her son mentioned that he was worried about an English test and was afraid he wouldn't graduate. She usually would have replied, "Oh, don't worry, you'll do fine." But this time, she remembered how she felt when her husband didn't seem to understand her feelings.

So she said to her son, "Why don't you get out your book and we'll go over it together?" They did, and afterward he said, "I think I'm going to do OK."

Once, I tried to discuss with a friend some decisions I needed to make. He went on and on about how I should do this and that. He wasn't helping me sort out what I wanted, he was deciding for me, and I resented it.

Then I realized I had done the same thing on many occasions. A friend told my sister that she didn't like to tell me anything she was thinking about doing because I would get excited about it and tell her everything I thought she should do. She felt guilty if she didn't follow my advice.

Until my sister related this conversation, I thought I was just being lovingly helpful. But with adults as well as children, we can be most helpful by listening with respect to them instead of jumping in with our own thoughts. Feeling our respect, they gain faith in their own ideas.

Even when they are shocking, we need to listen respectfully to our kids' ideas. They often will say things they don't mean, such as "Marijuana won't hurt you," just to get us on a subject they are worrying about.

If we ask them why they feel that way and get them to sort through their reasons without feeling threatened, they are more likely to listen to us afterwards. Our ideas, expressed logically in an aura of mutual trust, are much more likely to sink in.

Sometimes it's difficult to listen to the same problems over and over again, even when someone really needs us to. We want to say, "I'm really tired of hearing this."

But if someone is still going through something, those troubles are fresh to him, no matter how old they are to us.

I remember what a friend told me after I'd gone through a difficult time in my life. "You were really a pain, all those months," she said. "I got so tired of hearing the same old things, and I wished you'd do something about the situation instead of complaining about it."

I laughed, because it was over. But I'm glad she didn't tell me I was being a pain when I needed to talk. Because she listened with understanding, I was able to survive and, eventually, resolve my problems.

* * *

The women were talking about how they felt guilty when they didn't like someone.

"I really like most people," said the older woman. "But once in a while, I run into someone I simply can't stand. Usually it's someone who is two-faced or cruel or trying to rip other people off with some kind of a phony scheme. But even if I intellectually know they're not likable, I feel something's wrong with me because I can't like them."

The other woman laughed. "I know," she said. "And it's particularly upsetting when it's a member of your family—like my mother. She's always putting us kids down. We can't do anything right. And she tries to start fights between us—she'll repeat something my sister supposedly said about me and get me upset.

"Everytime I go to see her, I realize that I don't like my own mother, and then I'm depressed for days because I'm not supposed to feel like that."

Ah, but maybe we are supposed to "feel like that." If we enjoyed the company of those who make us feel bad about life, ourselves and others, we'd have to be masochistic. If we liked people who hurt others, we'd be at worst as bad as they are and at least insensitive.

We need to allow ourselves not to like some people. And that includes:

- People who put us down constantly.
- People who try to create problems for us, on our jobs, in our neighborhoods, between members of our family.
- People who demand too much of our time and attention—who make us feel continually guilty because no matter how much attention we give them, it's never enough.
- People who constantly talk gloom and doom, who are certain the world is headed for disaster and people are going to hell.
- People who put down other people, in the office, the home or on the street.
- People who incessantly complain that nobody is as sick, unhappy or mistreated as they are on the job, in their families, by the world in general.
- People who are cruel to others and who delight in creating trouble—consciously or unconsciously.

We get locked into the belief that we're supposed to keep giving to and be understanding of even the worst individuals. We think that because someone is old, miserable or a relative, we owe them time to inflict whatever misery they want on us.

We don't owe them that. We owe them brief

politeness if they're people we can't avoid entirely, such as family members. But we don't have to subject ourselves to whatever they dish out for as long as they want to dish it.

It's tempting to think that we can change someone we dislike by our behavior. If we only love them enough, they'll learn to love back. If we talk of hope when they mention despair, they'll brighten their outlook.

But it seldom works. The sad thing is that people change only when they see the need to change, and most unlikable people don't see that need.

As they reap the unhappiness they sow, we're not required to reap it with them. And we certainly shouldn't feel guilty about not liking them.

* * *

My friend had just been reading Og Mandino's book, *The Greatest Salesman in the World,* in which a salesman is given the secret to success: 10 scrolls, each with a different directive to be followed for 30 days.

This was the day she was going to follow the first directive: To be totally loving.

Before the morning was over, she had had to deal with several unreasonable customers and had to cut off a telephone conversation with a talkative family member so she could get some work done.

She was upset about the customers and sad that she couldn't give the time to the relative, who demanded constant attention from her.

"Where do you draw the line between being loving and being walked on?" she said.

It is difficult to know, but I believe:

- You are loving when you understand that your wife is having a rough time at work, so when she snaps at you, you respond by offering to rub her back.

• *You are walked on when your wife tells you she doesn't want you to take piano lessons because she thinks it's silly and you agree not to do it to make her happy, but you resent it.*

• You are loving when you realize that your husband wants to watch a special football game so you agree to keep him company.

• *You are walked on when you never ask your husband to spend a Sunday afternoon away from football doing what you want to do.*

• You are loving when you agree to help out your neighbor by taking him to work when his car is broken down.

• *You are walked on when you always drive your neighbor's kids and yours to baseball games because he hasn't offered to help out and you don't want to confront him about it.*

• You are loving when you give as much time as you have to church or club activities.

• *You are walked on when you give more time than you have because someone in the church or club will accuse you of not contributing.*

• You are loving when you agree to do something you don't want to do because you understand your boss really needs you to do it.

• *You are walked on when you don't ask for a raise or better working conditions because your boss might yell at you.*

• You are loving when you are pleasant and thoughtful with everyone you meet.

• *You are walked on when you let an unpleasant, unkind person keep you from saying or doing what you need to because you don't want to incur their wrath.*

• You are loving when you make your children do what they should do and when you say no to what they shouldn't do.

● *You are walked on when you let your children shout, cry and wear you down in an effort to get to do what they shouldn't and get out of doing what they should.*

● You are loving when you give people as much of your attention as you can.

● *You are walked on when you give people so much of your attention you can't get anything else done.*

Being loving is being considerate of other people. Being walked on is being afraid of other people.

Standing up, firmly but nicely, for what you really need and believe is being loving to yourself.

* * *

I was talking with a friend in a coffee shop the other evening when I looked out the window and saw an older couple head for a nearby restaurant, leaving their car lights on.

I jumped up in midsentence, raced out of the coffee shop and called to the couple. The man looked back at me.

"You left your lights on," I shouted.

"That's all right, dear," said the man. "They turn themselves off."

I turned to see a group of people laughing at me and the incident. Embarrassed, I walked back into the coffee shop and told my friend what had happened.

"You need to learn that it's not your job to take care of the whole world," he said.

I agree that it is not my job or anybody else's to take care of the whole world, but I believe we have a responsibility to take care of the small part of it that enters our lives.

For instance, even if we miss driving over the

broken glass in the shopping center parking lot, we can stop and pick it up so someone else won't drive over it.

We can carry our half-finished cup of pop out to the theater lobby so someone else won't knock it over when they are walking in the dark.

We can clean up the trash in the restroom sink so someone else does not have to face it like we did.

A friend of mine saw a package drop off a cart at the airport shortly before Christmas, and she talked to three different people before it was rescued and sent on its way.

"I couldn't stand to think of someone waiting for that package somewhere, and it wouldn't be there," she said.

While I was walking with another friend in a shopping mall one day, two women walked by, talking.

"I don't know if there is a toy store or not in this mall," one said to the other.

My friend interrupted them.

"There is one," she said and gave them directions. They smiled and thanked her.

My father always thought it was his job to take care of most of the world. I don't believe he ever passed up anyone stranded with a broken-down car by the side of the road.

He was always helping out neighbors, and when he sold real estate in a low-income area, he found ways to help financially strapped people get the furniture or household items they needed.

The rest of us may not be able to give as much as my father did. We may not have the time or resources to do all the things other people think we ought to, but we can do a great many little things that are right on our way through life.

A couple of nights after the coffee shop incident, my son and I went to a movie. We were getting in our car afterward when he suddenly got out and chased down a couple.

I immediately saw what had happened. They had left their car lights on. As I waited for him to return, I watched the car lights to see if they would go off, hoping he would not be embarrassed the way I had been.

However, he returned with a smiling man, who turned off his lights and then rejoined his wife.

I hope my son will continue to take care of the part of the world he comes across even if sometimes the car lights go off and people laugh.

I expect he will. After all, he is my father's grandson.

* * *

Two men walked past me in the hall. "I just went and bought..." the taller one started to say. "Some lottery tickets?" said the other. "I bought some, too, but I didn't win anything."

"No," the taller one said. "I decided to buy some..." "Trash bags?" the other said.

"No," the taller one said.

At that point they were too far away for me to hear any more of their conversation, so I never did learn what the taller man bought or why the shorter one jumped from the idea of lottery tickets to trash bags.

I was thinking about their conversation as I went past a co-worker's desk.

"I just heard something interesting in the hall," I said to her. "It made me stop and think that..."

"Oh, you saw that guy in the wild outfit, too," she said. "We were all talking about him."

"No, I didn't see him," I said. "Wait, maybe I did...was he wearing..."

"A red and white checkered jacket with green pants," she said. "Wasn't that crazy?"

"No, I didn't see him, but I did see some guy in . . ."

"A cowboy hat and boots?" she asked.

"Yeah, I saw him, too," I said, grateful we had finally come together on some information. "I heard him say he was up here to see about . . ."

"Probably some rodeo coverage," she said. "It's getting to be that time of year, I guess."

"No, no, he was here to see about a job," I said. "He wants to write . . ."

"Agriculture, probably, if you can judge by his outfit," she said.

"Actually, no. He's interested in doing features," I said. "He wrote for a paper . . ."

"Don't tell me . . ." she said. "Another transplant from the snowy Midwest."

"No, he's from a small California paper. I don't remember which one, but he seemed nice," I said.

"That's good," the co-worker said. "Speaking of nice, there's Ron. I need to ask him something."

She signaled to Ron, who walked over.

"I've been wanting to ask you about . . ." she said.

"All right, all right, don't jump all over me," Ron said. "I'm really sorry about that mix-up. It won't happen again."

"No," she said. "That's not what I wanted to talk about. I understand what happened. I need your help on something else."

"OK, but can it wait a minute?" he said. "I'm swamped right now. How about calling me this afternoon?"

As he walked off, the co-worker turned to me.

"Have you ever noticed how people have this irritating habit of . . ."

"Finishing what you're going to say before you say

it?" I asked.

"No," she said. "I meant..."

* * *

Many of our relationship problems stem from the fact we view our wives, husbands, children, employees or bosses as adversaries in a game we're playing.

This thought occurred to me after reading an article on violence in sports in *Psychology Today* magazine. The article explored how game "dynamics" allow moral people, who would not think of hitting their neighbors, to go into a football game, for instance, and physically destroy a member of the opposite team.

When asked if it was OK for a fictional football player called Tom to go in and injure his opponent, an athlete reasoned this way:

"If Tom looks at it as a game, it's OK to hurt the guy—to try to take him out of the game. But if he looks at the halfback as a person, and tries to hurt him, it's not OK...When you're on the field, then the game is football. Before and after, you deal with people morally."

The article then explored the idea that the same "game" philosophy, which sets up different moral standards, has been transplanted, along with sports language, to the business world and to politics. When we call a man an "opponent," it depersonalizes him, so we aren't hurting a person when we hurt the opponent, we are simply winning the game.

This opponent image is useful when we need to rally a nation to battle. The faceless-group image of the "enemy" makes it easier to go to war against individuals who would, taken one at a time, look a lot like our brothers, or sisters, neighbors or friends.

But we can go beyond the boardroom and the

political backrooms with this depersonalizing of the opponent; we can go straight into our bedrooms.

Think of the times you have heard, for instance, "the battle of the sexes" or "the war between men and women."

It begins in childhood with "girls can't play ball" or "boys are mean." It continues through life where men shut women out of conversations because "they wouldn't understand politics," or extremists in the women's movement see all men as the enemy, or a man uses his fists to subdue an impertinent wife.

Sadly, you see evidence of this opponent mentality in the results of a recent survey in which 70 percent of the teenage boys said it was all right to lie to a girl and say you loved her to get her to sleep with you.

The girl is not a girl. She is an adversary who has to be conquered, no matter what tactics you use. Girls do the same thing when they pretend to like something they don't or be something they are not to win a boy's affections.

Parents and children often view each other as the enemy, too. Teenagers particularly feel this. They are commonly referred to as a group: teenagers do this, teenagers do that, as though they all had one face, one personality.

Whenever we decide a whole segment of our population is exactly alike just because they share one characteristic, such as skin color or religious beliefs, we're in trouble.

When we see them as a large group with one face and not as individuals with many faces, like our own, it's easy to call them the enemy, particularly if we have had one bad experience with a member of the group and decide the whole group is that way.

Once we decide they are the enemy the rules change. We are now playing a game and the morality is different: We can lie, we can even use violence because we have convinced ourselves the only moral thing to do now is win.

* * *

He was a disreputable-looking character, lingering there behind the bench at the downtown bus stop. His hair was uncombed, his face unshaven. His clothes were unwashed and ill-fitting.

I prepared to give him wide berth as I walked by when suddenly he smiled.

The object of his appreciation was a toddler, leaning over the back of the bench. The man bent forward, talking to the baby in gentle tones, and the child responded, waving his arms and talking excitedly.

For a few moments they enjoyed each other. The baby didn't see the dirty garments or ungroomed hair I had judged the man by. He only saw his smile.

Chapter 9

I am not the me I appear to be

She had awakened that morning feeling overweight, unattractive and older than her 43 years. And that feeling had not lessened by the time she picked up a newspaper and ordered coffee at her favorite restaurant.

Then, a man from her past walked in and changed her day.

She had known him in school and had seen him only briefly a couple of times since, but this morning he stopped to drink coffee and talk.

He had changed and looked older, but he still had the same sunny smile and summer-sky blue eyes.

They talked mostly about the present: his wife and children, her children, his job and her job. However, seeing him took her back to the teenage girl she had been.

She had entertained crushes on him off and on through grammar and high school, but feelings were never returned. Then in her senior year came her big chance. They were cast as girlfriend and boyfriend in a high school comedy. The script called for a kiss at the end, but the teacher eliminated it as too risque for those innocent days.

Even without the kiss, it was a time of high romance for her. She awoke each morning anticipating the times they would be alone practicing their lines. And, occasionally, he gave her rides home from evening rehearsals.

Nothing was ever said, but she felt sometimes that he liked her, too. Then, she would tell herself that was impossible. After all, he was going steady with her girlfriend, who was sought after by all the boys in school. How could he like her, a shy girl who seldom dated?

Sometimes things he said or ways he looked made her continue to dream. And she did not feel guilty because she knew something he did not. Her girlfriend was not only going steady with him, but was engaged to a sailor and was dating a third guy on the side.

The weeks passed, however, and nothing happened. The rehearsals stopped, and the play began. With each performance, she saw her romantic dream fading without chance of a happy ending. Soon there would be no reason to get together.

During the final performance, she sadly played for the last time the role of girlfriend that she longed for in real life. Then, in the final moments of the final act, he grabbed her and kissed her.

The audience of mostly high school students exploded with catcalls and applause. The incident was written up in the school newspaper.

Despite knowing she would not spend any more time with him, she enjoyed her brief moment as the heroine of a romantic drama, one that had faded out properly with a kiss.

There was an epilogue. Years later, her girlfriend told her that she and her steady had a cleansing of the souls the summer after they all graduated.

Her friend confessed about the sailor fiance and other transgressions. He admitted that he had been romantically attracted to his stage girlfriend all those months they had rehearsed together.

Seeing him again this morning, the stage girlfriend thought of those moments of unrequited attraction and felt nostalgic affection for the adolescents they once were, struggling with love and conscience and growing up.

Nothing romantic passed between them on this morning 25 years later, and they might never meet again, but she suddenly felt more attractive, more happy.

A trip back into her youth had made her feel young again.

* * *

Maybe it is because I'm getting older, but I love it that so many women from Gloria Steinem to Joan Collins are telling their age proudly.

Fifty is sexy, 50 is smart, 50 is a great place in life to be. They are paraphrasing Steinem's statement of 10 years ago, saying, "This is what 50 looks like. It looks good."

When on her 40th birthday, a reporter remarked, "You don't look 40," Steinem replied, "This is what 40 looks like. We've been lying for so long, who would know?"

Many of my friends are still lying about their ages. One of them says, jokingly, "A woman who will tell her age will tell anything."

That remark has cleverly cloaked her age for years. I don't even know how old she is.

Another woman, who is single, has given her age as

35 for years because she says that once a man finds out you're older than 35, he isn't interested. Perhaps. But, I think a man who finds you attractive until you tell him you are 40 is too shallow to be of interest to any thinking woman.

I hate to admit, however, that I'll think someone is quite young until he tells me his age.

Then, I unconsciously look for some lines around the eyes, some gray in the hair. And, in spite of myself, the person looks a little older to me.

Perhaps we would all be better off if we just didn't tell our ages—any of us. Then others won't look for extra lines in our faces and decide we're not desirable as marriage partners or too far over the hill for management promotions.

People are such different ages at any age, anyway. I know people of 40 who act as if their lives are over and people of 70 who awake each day with the same zest for living they had at 25.

But, while I'm advocating that we stop judging age altogether, I admit I'm flattered, when someone says I don't look my age. I suddenly feel better about myself. Young, I believe, is more attractive than old. After all, I'm a product of our youth-oriented culture, too.

But think of it this way, if they say I look 10 years younger than I am, they're taking away 10 years of my life: 10 years when I did more growing as a person than during any prior decade.

Ten years in which I raised my children through adolescence to adulthood. Ten years in which I survived an age crisis, got out of a relationship that was destroying me, learned that management was not something I wanted to do and writing was something I had to do.

Ten years in which I learned to diet successfully,

learned to stop trying to get my friends to do things my way and quit looking to other people to tell me what to do with my life.

Ten years in which I made some special new friends, solidified relationships with old ones and found that my grandmother could be just as close to me after death.

Ten years in which I learned that I could handle things that life brought me so I began to worry less, trust more in tomorrow and enjoy today.

In August, I will be 44. At 34, I wasn't half the person I am now. When I am 54, I hope I'll be more than twice the person I now am.

And I can't wait to see what I'll be like at 94.

* * *

Money, age and sex rank right up there as subjects people lie about most, but I bet the big winner in the falsehood competition is food.

Dieters seldom tell you what they really ate.

"I only had an apple for lunch," a dieter will say, forgetting to mention that she had a midmorning snack of three doughnuts and a milkshake.

Or she will say, "This is all I am going to have to eat today," knowing full well she will slip just like she did the day before and binge on popcorn that evening.

Where calories are concerned, most of us tell the biggest lies to ourselves. Try asking anyone how many calories there are in their favorite foods, and they will quote you far fewer than there actually are: "This brownie isn't that big, and without frosting it's no worse than a small apple."

Some people judge the amounts they eat as though they were viewing them through the reverse end of a telescope. The other day I watched a man put away potato skins with sour cream and cheese, a bowl of soup, a salad, a steak, a baked potato, carrots and apple pie.

"That wasn't a large meal," he said later, insisting thin people regularly eat that way.

Many of us tell ourselves that, if a food is good for us, it won't make us fat. Or we tell ourselves that if it is low in calories, like yogurt, we can eat all we want of it.

We also have developed the theory that food is not going to get us at certain times. For instance, if our metabolism is speeded up by exercising, we can eat the chocolate cake, ice cream sundae and french fries. Exercise, we believe, will keep the fat from collecting on our hips.

Food tasted in the process of cooking is lower in calorie content, too, we've decided. After all, the cook is doing what is necessary, tasting to make sure it is good. She's virtuous.

In dieter annals, virtue negates calorie content. A person sitting down in front of the television and consuming a bowl of whipped cream deserves to get fat. Guilt requires it.

However, virtuous eating—like celebrating with a friend who got promoted or making your hostess happy or making yourself feel better because the boss is on your case—never gets you fat.

Many of us also hate to admit how often we eat fast food. There is still a mystique that the good mother cooks a big country meal and gathers her family around to ooh and aah over her heavily spread table while the oven emits wonderful smells of homemade bread and rhubarb pie.

A woman admitting she doesn't cook is tantamount to admitting she is not a real woman. So most women have a dish or two they can brag about making, as if they make this sort of thing every day.

That does not include a friend of mine who said she has discovered a simple way of getting out of making those required dishes for the office party, church potluck or family get-togethers.

"I just tell everyone I don't cook," she said. "You'd be amazed at how much time that saves you. Nobody expects you to contribute homemade dishes. They ask you to bring the potato chips or ice. And nobody expects you to invite them over for dinner. It's really liberating."

Now you may applaud this woman for being brave enough to be honest about her lack of culinary ability.

I hate to disappoint you. I have eaten many a sinfully tasty meal at her house. She is a great cook who has just found another way to lie about food.

* * *

At last, the experts are jogging around to my way of thinking: Exercise is bad for you.

Actually, I knew it already. At least, it was bad for me. It messed up my mind with guilt when I didn't do it. When I did do it, it messed up my relationships because I spent my evenings running instead of creating emotional closeness over dinner.

To be honest, my most consistent exercise was wrestling—wrestling with myself to exercise.

I bought a trampoline and jumped on it four days the first week, one day the second. That's all the use it got until I gave it to a friend.

I started a running program several times and stayed with it several weeks until it got too cold, too rainy, too hot or too hard to do when it seemed the rest of the world was lolling in front of the TV set with chips and dip.

I exercised with Jane Fonda on videotape for at least a month last spring. I haven't seen her since.

I thought about swimming regularly. I thought about it a lot.

I also thought strenuously about bicycle riding. My thought muscles are in great shape.

While looking for ways to make myself exercise, I also looked for reasons not to. And I thought I found the perfect excuse when I saw a newspaper ad for a health club. The woman in the ad was all bone and muscle and no curves. Nowhere.

"That does it," I told a friend in the office. "I don't want to look like that."

This friend and I are always talking about exercising, and it tells you something about how well we follow through when our tongues are in better shape than the rest of our bodies.

He didn't buy my argument that the skinny woman in the ad was a good excuse to give up the thought of exercising. He was too busy measuring the girth of his stomach with his hands and citing the magical thinning powers of running.

Although I couldn't enlist him in my campaign to rid myself of guilt, I didn't give up hope. I knew how all those researchers produce results one day that prove something is great for your health and then come out a couple of years later with evidence that it's bad for your health. I was certain research would eventually vindicate my exercise sit-in.

Sure enough, just the other day, Dr. Henry Solomon, a cardiologist, came out with a book, *The Exercise Myth,* which warns people against strenuous exercise. Solomon said studies show that exercise has nothing to do with the reason people live longer, and it can even be dangerous. He said the chance of death during vigorous exercise is seven to nine times higher than if you're just lying around.

In fact, Dr. Solomon said a lack of stress in your life is the most likely factor to make you live longer.

So get off my back, all you running addicts. You're endangering my life with your stress-producing so-called healthful advice.

Just think of me as the tortoise, ambling comfortably toward the finish line—at least, until some other expert refutes what this expert says and I have to wrestle with guilt once again.

* * *

"I think I'll take the new body out for a test run and see what it will do," said a woman who had lost 30 pounds.

It's doing very well. Men who ignored her when she was heavier are asking her to dance.

She is more confident, too, about asking men to dance because she's less afraid they are going to reject her, she said. However, not all of the fear is gone. Her new slimness has its drawbacks.

"I've realized that I've been hiding behind my weight. I could tell myself, 'If they don't like me, it's because of my weight,'" she said. "Now, if they don't like me, it's because of me. That's scary."

Off and on over the last several years, I've talked to lots of women about being overweight. While there are as many reasons for gaining and keeping weight as there are women. I've discovered that many wrap themselves in extra pounds as a protection of some kind.

Many times, it appears to be a protection from the opposite sex. But if you look closely, it's protection from themselves.

Two women I know admit that part of the reason they gained weight was to help protect themselves from their sexual feelings. They were afraid that if they were too attractive to men, they would be tempted to indulge in sexual relationships they wouldn't feel good about.

One woman is afraid she would be unfaithful to her husband if she lost weight. So she saves her marriage by eating.

The other has problems dealing with her sexual desires because she grew up believing that only bad girls liked sex. By overeating, she keeps herself from thinking about sex because she believes no one would be interested in loving her anyway. Fat helps her remain a "good" girl.

Not all overweight women, of course, are hiding from sex; but once they talk to counselors about it, some discover they are. Others, like the first woman, who feared rejection, may be protecting themselves from something else.

One woman admitted after some serious soul-searching that she is holding onto her weight because she fears that if she became too attractive she would get out of her marriage. Staying overweight keeps her believing that no one but her husband would want her and keeps her from having to face that decision.

Another woman said her husband had never been as interested in sex as she was, even in the early days of their marriage, when she was svelte. Now, she knows she keeps the extra weight on because she can blame it for the fact that he doesn't want to make love.

When she feels sexy, she eats instead. It does double duty: She's so full she doesn't feel like making love; and she can tell herself that the fat is the reason he doesn't like her, and that when she loses weight, everything will be all right. Thus she puts off dealing with the real problem of their unequal sexual desires.

Other women said they had realized they were staying fat so they didn't have to look for a job or a man. They had to lose weight, they told themselves, before they could do what they should do. So they started diets, then quickly sabotaged them and continued to put off risking rejection.

One woman said a dream made her realize she was staying overweight for protection.

She dreamed she and her brother were leading a fat cow through a field. The field was wet, and her feet kept sinking in. Then, all of a sudden, she was in water up to her shoulders.

"When did we get into the river?" she asked her brother.

But she wasn't afraid. The water was warm, and it swirled about her comfortingly. She felt safe.

In analyzing the dream the next day, she immediately recognized that her weight did that for her. It was comforting; it felt safe.

Chapter 10
Perfect in our imperfection

My friends, Monday is Valentine's Day, and you probably already have purchased gifts and cards for those you love.

To your mother you have written, "I love you. Thank you for all the wonderful things you've done for me."

For your father you have purchased a card that wraps your love for him in humor, and you will give it to him with a kiss.

To your sister you have sent a bouquet of flowers thanking her for all the close conversation, the support in rough times, the sharing in good times.

For your husband or wife you plan a special dinner, a thoughtfully chosen gift, a sentimental card and an evening reveling in all the wonderful reasons you chose him or her.

And after you have thought of all these special people and all the things you love about them, your mind returns to its usual pastime—punishing you for not measuring up to other people's expectations or your own.

"You're too fat, too lazy, too short-tempered, too stupid," you say to yourself. It is your favorite litany.

You start the day by looking in the mirror and groaning and end the day by sticking your head in the pillow and worrying about all the things you should have done but didn't, or all the things you should not have done but did.

This holiday, would you not do that? Would you instead take time to give a valentine to yourself?

You are not only the flawed person you see in your mind and mirror. You are also the person who wants your children to be happy, who loves your mothers, who tries to do well at your job, who takes care of your pets and helps your neighbor.

You are the person who cares enough to want to be better, to become wiser, more disciplined, more understanding of other people. So on your valentine, would you list all the good things about you?

Start with how you look, your best features. The things your husband loves or your wife has complimented you on. You may be overweight, but you have lovely hair. You may be out of shape, but you have sexy eyes.

Then list all the compliments you have received lately, when you wore your new suit, made that amazing return in tennis or presented an innovative idea in the staff meeting.

Then write down all the things you do for other people, the meals you fix, the gifts you give, the telephone calls you make. Include the time you spend teaching your son to shoot a basket, your daughter to ride a bike, your nephews how to beat you at video games.

Include the drives to the store with your mother or grandmother, the dinners out with a friend who is lonely, the times you said a prayer for someone you didn't know when an ambulance passed you in the street.

Include all these things, my friends. Keep writing all day, as you think of more, as you do more. Keep the list to read on those days when you think you are not needed, you are not contributing, you are not worthwhile.

It will remind you of what a lot of people who know you have realized for a long time:

You are special, you are lovable and you are somebody's very necessary valentine, every day.

* * *

Human needs and angers are a dark and surprising bunch.

They are never more traumatic than when they make you do something you never believed you could do.

It has happened to me enough over my lifetime to make me humble. Whenever I'm feeling a little smug about growing into a more understanding, less judgmental person—whenever I think I'm getting to be downright good—I manage to do something that makes me realize how much I have to grow.

Those experiences help me remember, when I hear of or see something terrible someone else has done, that "there but for the grace of God go I."

Is it possible, for instance, that, but for that "grace," any one of us could have been born into a situation that might have made us a child or spouse abuser?

Is it possible that we could face a circumstance that would make us a murderer? That conditions could be so threatening that we could pick up a gun and shoot someone?

Is it possible, but for that "grace," that we could be so hurt and frustrated that we would take it out on everyone around us?

Is it possible that because of a combination of circumstances, we could throw away a career and find ourselves cradling a bottle on skid row?

While most of us don't go to those extremes, we can reach points in our lives when we fall over the edge of rationality into the darker places of our nature and do something we thought we would never do. We also see those dark deeds in the people around us.

A sister is unfaithful to her husband. A child chooses a socially unacceptable lifestyle. A friend betrays a trust. A co-worker breaks company rules. A neighbor spreads vicious gossip about a friend. A brother says something that destroys a vulnerable family member.

What do you do when these things happen? Can you forgive these people for being fallible human beings?

A more difficult concern is what you should do if you are the one who did these things. Do you sentence yourself to a permanent hell, or do you find a way to forgive yourself, vow to learn from the experience and go on?

Everyone makes mistakes. If we all stopped in our tracks, rooted in permanent regret, we would never love again, give again, create again, enjoy again.

Sometimes, when we are hurt by someone, we would like to be able to see that person never create again or enjoy again. We enjoy the idea of an eternal hell, and if God won't provide it for them, we would be glad to.

But as long as we hold onto our anger and hatred—as long as we brood on the hurt—we are just as much in prison as they are. Sometimes more so. The other person may have moved on, but we are still dwelling in the pain of unforgiveness.

Those people who seem to find it impossible to

forgive others tend to be the ones who hate the weaknesses they see in themselves. So if we can reach back to times we made serious mistakes and forgave ourselves, it will become easier now to see others as fallible human beings, just like us, and forgive them.

When we are the transgressor—when we are lost in remorse and guilt—we need to remember that we have a lot of company in those dark irrational places in our lives. And we need to remind ourselves that permanent pennance helps no one. It immobilizes you and makes everyone around you miserable.

The sooner we can forgive ourselves and others for being all too human, the sooner we can get back to the important business of growing again.

* * *

She looked across the breakfast table at him on Wednesday and thought: "If he gives me one more negative comment on the state of the world and how everything is going to hell, I'm going to scream, I don't think I can stand living with this constant downer anymore. What's with him, anyway? He used to be a lot more fun. Now he just complains all the time."

She looked across the breakfast table at him on Friday:

"He is such a doll. We had such a good time last night. He is so thoughtful and so sweet—when I think about the things some people have to put up with, with their husbands. . . I'm so lucky to have him. I am feeling so good about everything today."

She looked across the breakfast table at him on Saturday:

"Oh, it's difficult to realize he's getting so much older. What if something happens to him and I have to live without him? I couldn't stand it; it would be awful. I've got to quit thinking like this, it's just making me miserable."

The woman was laughing at herself as she talked with me about the three mornings and her different attitudes toward her husband.

"I realized, all of a sudden, the only thing that had really changed in all of those three mornings was my perception of him and our relationship," she said.

"I was angry at him and so he was unlovable, and I spent the whole day being irritated and literally wishing he would go away. Then I felt good toward him, so he was wonderful and I couldn't get enough of his company.

"Then I started to worry about what might happen, and so I couldn't be happy with him because I was so worried about losing him."

As we talked about this matter of perception, I mentioned something that had happened to me recently.

I told a friend that when I looked at my daughter's wedding pictures, I could hardly enjoy them because I looked so awful in them.

"I looked so fat and so old!" I said.

The friend looked at me and asked, "Who says old and fat is bad?"

"Well, society does, for one thing," I said. "If you're old, you are less attractive, have less value. The same with being fat."

"Wait," she said, "you are the one who has told yourself that being old and fat is bad. It is your view of it. If you saw old and fat as good, then it wouldn't matter what society thinks of it."

She's right. And if every one of us who is getting older started proclaiming how proud we are of our years, maybe we could change society's perception of old as bad.

We reinforce that perception by refusing to tell our ages, as if admitting we're getting older is telling something shameful.

I appreciated it the other night when singer Anne Murray began her concert at Grady Gammage Center by announcing that she is 41 and feeling good about it. Then she named the reasons she felt good, among them that her legs looked great and her voice sounded great.

Later, after a particularly demanding song, she commented, "That's what you do when you're 41: You sing your buns off!"

I'm sure most people in the audience, laughing with her, felt good about her age, and a little better about theirs, too.

I watch friends worry about turning 25, 30 or 40. I know the fear because I've been there.

But on the whole, I've never been happier. My life has become better with every year.

One morning last week, I drove to work playing Billy Joel's *Modern Woman* with a cool morning breeze blowing through the car's sun roof, and I felt wonderful about my life and myself. Another morning, I drove to work, feeling lousy. Nothing changed. Just my perception.

* * *

My sister and I were talking about how we keep wanting to solve every problem for ourselves and our family. And how we want to wrap up all our lives in neat little packages of perfection.

We want the answers, now and permanently. A brother gets the great job and is happy forever. A niece gets her degree and is successful forever. A nephew marries the perfect person and is loved forever.

Every crisis solved, every life tied up with ribbons of success.

But life doesn't cooperate. It keeps throwing things at you and the people you love. A perfect job goes sour; so does a perfect marriage. Illness changes the direction of a career; so does a financial disaster. Some problems, like a physical disability, have no answer.

Even when you think you have the answers, the people you love seldom listen. For instance, my sister found the right man for her daughter; I found the right girl for my son. But her daughter had her own ideas and my son had his own, too.

It's frightening, we agreed. They might marry the "wrong" person and suffer. They may even end up divorced.

Then we laughed ruefully at ourselves. Here we were wanting to ensure a smooth road for our children, even though we had often talked about how grateful we were for the problems in our lives. We were proud of how expertly we had negotiated the bumps and how much we had grown in understanding. But we would deny our children the same chance to make choices, to make mistakes, to grow and feel good about it.

Adult children who haven't experienced problems would be as bland and undeveloped as mannequins, we agreed. Those people who have had it easy are not only the least interesting but are often the most judgmental.

If they've never had a problem child, it may be difficult for them to understand how even the best parents can watch their sweet 10-year-old become an angry drug addict at 15. If they've been lucky enough to marry a loving man or woman, they can find it easy to judge that a person who ended an unloving marriage "just didn't work hard enough at it."

While it's true that my sister and I know people who have been embittered by a life of hardship, we also know others who are mellowed by it. Those people we like best have usually suffered reverses and made mistakes.

But knowing that our relatives need to learn from their problems and to make their own decisions about their lives doesn't stop my sister and me from what we term "loving interference." After all, we were raised on the belief that family members help each other, and we have been helped by the family.

So we go through the names of brothers and sisters, children and parents one by one, thinking of what we can give in the way of time, encouragement or gifts that will make them feel better about themselves and help them get what they want.

Occasionally, when we arrive at an idea that appears to work, we rejoice. But we're getting wiser. We're beginning to realize that dealing with life's difficulties is like stamping out brush fires: Another will spring up and then another.

So we're learning not to frustrate ourselves with the goal of permanent solutions and perfectly packaged lives. We're just glad for today's answer; tomorrow we'll work on another one.

* * *

Have you ever had a day when you could not say the right thing?

You ask a question in a meeting and it sounds so dumb you wish you could take it back.

You agree to give a speech to a group of teenagers, and when you're there, you realize nothing you say is going to make them want to listen.

You make what is meant to be a clever comment to someone in the hall, and it comes out sounding like a putdown.

You tell someone you can't do something, and it appears you're telling him you don't want his company.

You ask a woman who is wearing a smock when her baby is due and find out she isn't pregnant.

You try to talk to your child about something important, and you sound preachy, not understanding.

You try to talk to your spouse about something important, and you sound critical, not concerned.

You tell a co-worker you liked his article, and he says he thought it was awful and he wished he had not had his name on it.

You tell your boss about something that happened that you are proud of, and you sound as if you are bragging.

You tell a friend about something you have accomplished, and you discover she tried to do it, too, and failed.

You talk to an irate person on the telephone, and instead of soothing them, you make them angrier because you sound condescending.

You go to a friend's house and her mother answers the door, and you say "Is anyone home?" meaning your friend or her husband.

You tell somebody how wonderful he looks since he has lost weight, and you find out he is ill.

You tell the church you can't teach Sunday School because you have this, this and this to do, and you end up sounding as if you are just making excuses.

You tell a friend you had a great weekend, and she says she wishes you had called her because hers wasn't so great.

You tell a co-worker you thought the humor in a given movie was really adolescent, and he says he thought it was one of the funniest movies he has seen.

You express your concern about how tired a co-worker looks, and she replies she hadn't felt tired until you mentioned it.

You call someone for a favor and mention how much you appreciated a recent favor, and he seems so happy you called until you mention the added favor. You wish you had just thanked him and forgot it.

You tell someone her hair looks great, and she says she was planning to get it cut because it looked so awful.

You are called on in class, and you give the wrong answer because you didn't hear the question.

You answer the phone and respond to a question with "Yes, ma'am" and the caller replies, "I'm a sir, not a woman."

And have you ever written something that didn't say quite what you meant to say so that instead of laughing or understanding, people got angry?

Oh, I have.

* * *

The 2-year-old girl watched her mother cuddle the newborn baby to her breast. Only a few days ago, she had been the only baby in her mother's life; she had been the only one her father had been eager to pick up and hold when he came home from work.

Now this intruder was getting the love that had been hers. How could she get it back? How could she make sure her parents would love her?

Her mother looked over at her. "Hand me a diaper, honey, please," she said.

When the child carried over the diaper, the mother smiled at her affectionately.

"Thank you, honey," she said. "You're such a good girl."

And then the child knew. She would be the perfect helper and her mother would smile. As long as she was a good girl, her mother and father would not stop loving her.

This little vignette is not about one particular person, but about people—and I know many—who at some point in their lives decided that the way to get and keep love was to meet the standards of perfection set by those around them.

I call it the A-student syndrome, and it manifests itself in many ways. You see it in the first-grader who cries when she misses a question on a test and in the teenager who feels guilty if he gets a B-plus.

You see it in the woman who will not go anywhere unless her hair is perfectly done. "I couldn't stand anyone seeing me like this," she says. She might not get an A in appearance; she might not be loved.

You see it in the man who feels he has to solve all the family's problems. If his brother needs a car, he must find it for him. If his mother needs more attention, he must provide it. If a niece's boyfriend needs a job, he will give him one.

No matter how many people make demands on his time and pocketbook, he must meet those demands. If he can't, he no longer will be the perfect helper.

You see the A-student syndrome in people who want to be perfect parents, perfect friends, perfect athletes or artists. There is a tension in them, as if they are ever striving after something they haven't quite claimed.

And they will never claim it. For each time an A student receives an A, he has little time to rejoice because another test of his perfection is coming.

So if he pleases one teacher, one time, he cannot rest. He must go on to please another teacher another time. If he pleases one person, there always is another person who might question his perfection. So he has to measure up, again and again.

Because standards of perfection vary so widely, there is no way he can win an A from everyone. A painting loved by one man is hated by another. A song that touches one woman's heart means nothing to another. A way of doing things that seems efficient to one boss seems a waste of time to another.

So the A student's effort to measure up on every test by every person can drive him crazy in the long run. Some have nervous breakdowns; others react by not trying anything anymore because it's easier not to take the test than to get less than an A.

However, the lucky ones learn that they do not have to measure up to others' standards to be worthwhile. They realize that those who truly love them will do so even when they don't meet accepted standards.

They know, at last, that each person is closest to perfect when he is completely and comfortably himself.

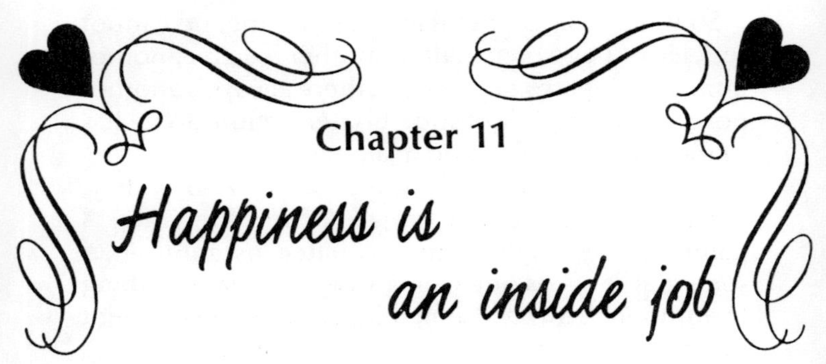

Chapter 11
Happiness is an inside job

My daughter turned 25 this week. It doesn't seem possible she is that age or that it's so long since I was that age.

I remember being 25. I had two children: Kim, 4 and Rick, 1. My husband was out of work; we didn't even have a shoestring to live on.

I went back to work, and what I remember most is constantly being tired and constantly worrying. Worrying about money, worrying about child care, worrying about whether I was giving the job I loved and the family I loved the best I could give them.

I was a little like the greyhound at the race track, chasing an elusive prize. The goal of feeling good and peaceful, of being in control of my life the way I wanted to be was always just ahead of me, no matter how fast I ran after it.

I see much of that racing in my daughter. She doesn't have children yet, but she's working and going to school and planning a wedding and trying to keep her fiance happy and making sure she remembers family and friends on each birthday and holiday.

She worries about money, about doing well in school, about getting a career started, getting a home started, getting a family started and about making everything work out right. She wants it all to be perfect; she wants to make an A-plus in everything.

Poor kid. She inherited that. It's only in the past few years that I've been able to relax a little and feel good about getting B's in some things.

It's this learning to relax a little that makes me glad I'm 20 years older than my daughter. In those 20 years I've realized it's all right to make mistakes and to accept with equanimity the mistakes of others. The world, both larger and personal, is never going to be perfect, no matter how much you race around. A better asset than energy for getting through life is a sense of humor and an ability not to hold things too tightly.

Laughing comfortably at yourself and the idiosyncracies of other people, finding the fun in tedious things and the hidden humor in dark situations will keep you more mentally healthy than any psychologist, self-help book or miracle pill.

Combine laughter with the realization that change is the natural order of life, and you're in good shape to survive happily into old age. You can't hold onto anything permanently so the sooner you learn to let go and move on, the happier you'll be.

Books get lost, your favorite dress wears out, your youth fades, friends move away, parents die and your children come into life to leave you. Eventually, you understand that the only thing you can really hold onto is a peaceful center somewhere inside you that connects with something greater than yourself.

All these things I've learned since I was 25. That's why when a friend looked at Kim the other day and said, "Oh, don't you wish you were that age again with your whole life before you?" I replied, "Absolutely not."

If anything, I wish I could on this birthday give my daughter all the things I learned in the 20 more years I've lived. I wish I could spare her the hard times, the awakenings that I know she'll have to go through before she discovers she doesn't have to race so hard to be happy.

But then, perhaps, that would deny her the pleasure of discovery, the satisfaction of knowing and conquering the territory herself. And feeling good, 20 years later, about how far she's come.

* * *

A woman I know writes an excellent column on feelings and family for a throwaway shopper in a Midwestern town. For some time I have been encouraging her to try writing for one of the major papers there.

But she won't. She's not sure she could write several columns a week, she said. Now, she only writes two a month.

Sure, you can, I told her. Sometimes it is easier to write several a week because your mind is always on column writing—you get in a habit of thinking "column"—you look at everything in the light of whether it would be column material.

Well, she is not sure the "more sophisticated audience" of the larger paper would like what she writes, she said.

It would be the same type of people reading your column in a larger paper, I said. Just more of them.

Well, she just is not sure she has that much to say, she said. A minister she admired told her that people should not write until they had something to say.

I asked if the minister gives a sermon every week. I bet he thinks of something to say each week because he has to, I said. You would be surprised by how much you have to say, if you know you have to write something and put your mind to it.

Besides, I added, if you don't have something to say at 50, do you think you'll have more at 60? Actually, as you get older, you never feel you know everything you should. If anything, the more you learn, the more you realize how little you do know. So, if you are waiting until you know everything to write or say something, it will never happen.

Well, she just doesn't think she is ready yet.

Oh, how often I've heard that: "I'm not ready yet."

What it means is: "I don't really want to do it because if I do, I might fail. This way, I can enjoy the success of people complimenting me on my potential, without putting myself on the line and proving I can do it or, worse, can't do it.

"And, if I were honest, about it, I really don't want you or anyone else telling me to put myself on the line. I'm perfectly happy here, thinking I could do it if I really wanted to. It's safe. It's satisfying."

To help maintain this safe and satisfying position, people create a thousand excuses:

- "My husband won't let me."
- "I don't have the time right now, my job is too demanding."
- "I write every day for a living, it's impossible to go home and write a book in the evenings."
- "When the children are grown, I will."
- "When I retire, I will."
- "When I finish this project, I will."
- "I need to finish college first."
- "I need to lose weight and get myself in shape first."
- "I need to get the house remodeled first."

All of these are good excuses—and I have used many of them myself—but the safest is "I'm not ready yet," because it is open-ended. There comes a time when college is finished, the house is remodeled and the kids are grown and you have to make good on your promise to try. But "I'm not ready yet" can carry you safely through the years from 15 to 96.

It sounds good because it implies that you are a wise person who knows better than to tackle something you have not matured enough to handle or have not carefully prepared for. But, down deep, you know it is simply a cover-up for "I'm afraid."

* * *

At first he loved managing the little camera shop. He had always been fascinated with cameras and photography, and he liked passing on his enthusiasm to the people who came into the shop.

In fact, he liked working with people even more than he liked dealing with camera equipment. He enjoyed showing them how to use different models, helping them improve their pictures and decide what kind of equipment they needed. Sometimes, he would talk them out of buying an expensive camera when a less expensive one would suit them as well.

In the morning, he looked forward to going to work early to be well-prepared for his customers. They were few at first, but he didn't mind. He felt confident that business would grow and he enjoyed being able to spend time and make friends with each one.

People began coming back to him because, as one person said, "It just makes me feel good to come in here." They also began telling their friends about how nice and helpful he was and how reliable his products were. Those friends came and sent their friends.

Soon he could no longer handle it all himself. He had to hire salespeople. Then he had to expand the store and hire more people.

Gradually, the job became less and less fun. He had to direct and discipline his help. He fired some, hired more. The expansion of the store brought added financial problems and more extensive book work. He began spending his time dealing with personnel and financial problems and seldom saw his customers.

Once in awhile, when he was out on the floor, someone would say to him, "Hey, where have you been, I've been here several times and hadn't seen you. I wanted to show you some great pictures I took with that camera you sold me."

He would respond cogenially, but briefly. He didn't have time to talk, there was too much to do. He was working nights and weekends to get it done.

One day, he realized he hated his job because it gave him no free time with his family, because it seemed to be nothing but a series of management headaches, but mostly because it was depriving him of what he enjoyed most: dealing directly with the public.

He talked to a friend about giving up management and going back to selling. The friend, a manager in a large company, grinned wryly and said, "Can't take the pressure like the rest of us, huh?"

He tried to explain that he wasn't afraid of management, he just didn't like it. But he realized that if he quit, people would judge him a quitter.

He wondered that about himself. Was he copping out by going back to doing something that didn't pay as well, but he enjoyed more?

He talked it over with his wife. "I don't see it as copping out," she said. "I think it's courageous to make a decision that will make you happier, despite what other people think you should or shouldn't do."

Months later, after much agonizing, he made the decision to go back to selling.

"I've redefined success," he said. "I used to think it was becoming more and more powerful and making more and more money. Now I know success is being able to make a living at something you love to do and having the guts to turn down power and money to do it."

* * *

Driving to work the other morning, I listened to a new song I like. When it was over, I wanted to rewind the tape and listen to it again, but I felt I shouldn't because I might get tired of the song too soon.

Later, I realized I tend to do the same thing with clothes. If I really like an outfit, I won't wear it often enough to get tired of it.

I think it comes from when I was growing up, and my family couldn't afford new clothes too often. I rationed each new dress by wearing it only occasionally, so I wouldn't get tired of it and could look forward to wearing it again.

New records were also a luxury, so I didn't wear out the songs on the one I got for Christmas by playing them too often.

Now, when I can afford to buy new clothes and new records whenever I feel like it, I'm still rationing. I wear clothes I don't like and listen to music I don't like because I am still saving the ones I really like.

"Make it last" was the watchword at our house. So we mended old clothing, cut rotten places out of fruit and repaired autos and appliances over and over again. It was sacrilegious to replace something, no matter how often it broke.

Even when we had to buy something, we believed a good person bought old, not new. We got bargains and then made them over to work for us.

All of this is fine when you really need to save money, but it can hinder you when you are poorer in time than in funds.

One woman I know spends hours each week clipping coupons, even though she earns more in an hour at work than she saves by using coupons at the grocery store. Then she complains about not having time to get everything done.

There are times when I'm able to throw out my childhood worry about money and take real pleasure in it. Once, a friend and I drove to Los Angeles to see a play and drove back the next day.

Recently, my sisters, mother and I chipped in to fly another sister in from Denver for the day so she could attend a seminar with us. We had a great time.

It was impractical, of course, to pay the plane fare for just one day here. But, partly for that reason, it was more special and something I know we'll never forget.

In this exploration of my "save" consciousness, I am taking a look at my tendency to save boxes and old wrapping paper to put gifts in. My family has a joke that you can never tell what a gift is by the box, because perfume is apt to be wrapped in a camera box.

I also have realized that I hate to give up any free magazine or book I get, even if I don't really want to read it.

I was taught not to waste anything. Books must be read. Clothes must be worn. Things must be used. Even if you don't really want them.

I am recognizing that it is a subconscious lack of faith in the future. I can't enjoy things today, or give them away if I don't want them, because there might not be anything there for me to enjoy tomorrow. I may not get anything. I may not be able to afford anything. So I've got to hold on to what I've got today.

After I thought about it, I decided I didn't want to live that way. It takes too much enjoyment out of life. As I drove home that night, I listened to the song I liked four times.

It was true that after listening that night and six times the next morning I didn't want to hear the song again. But it was great fun while it lasted.

And I just discovered another song I really like.

* * *

In her novel *The Accidental Tourist,* Anne Tyler paints a picture of a man who carefully has protected himself from life's vagaries with routine and systems for doing everything. Or so he thinks.

But even washing his clothes in the bathtub as he showers can't protect him from his son dying or his wife leaving. By carefully avoiding conversation with seatmates on plane trips, he wraps himself in a cocoon of safety, only to find it is mummifying him.

Then he learns, with the help of an unconventional woman he doesn't like at first, to enjoy life's odd offerings, even when they are slightly uncomfortable. He also learns to go after things he wants instead of letting things happen to him.

By choosing her and her life full of colorful people, he chooses the discomfort of the unconventional and unexpected over the easier way of order and conventionality.

"I suppose you realize what your life is going to be like," his ex-wife says. "You'll be one of those mismatched couples no one invites to parties. No one will know what to make of you. People will wonder whenever they meet you, 'My God, what does he see in her?' "

"I'm sorry, Sarah," he replies. "I didn't want to decide this." He, too, knows it would be much easier to stay in a nest, comfortably furnished with the expected.

It's easier to curl up and watch TV than to dress up and fight traffic to enjoy a concert or play. It's easier to spend the weekend in the back yard instead of climbing Squaw Peak.

But then you don't get the panorama of mountains and city or the pride in mastering a mountain. You also don't get the sweat, the aching muscles, the dust of desert and rock.

Those who live well realize that when you choose to look for life's surprises, you get the accompanying drawbacks. When you camp out, you get bugs, snakes, rocks in the backbone. But you also get starry skies, sweet scent of dew-dampened pine and invigorating freshness of morning air.

When you go to a party, you may meet boredom or rejection. You also may meet a person who lights up your evening, or your life.

When you swim in the ocean, you get seaweed around your legs and salt in your eyes. You also get the exhilaration of cold water, the excitement and power of the waves.

When you have a relationship with an exciting person, you get the discomfort of knowing the rest of the world finds him or her exciting, too, and you could lose that person.

When you have a relationship with anyone, you get the discomfort of little irritations—the fact that you often can't do things exactly when and how you'd like. But you get the warmth, the sharing, the loving moments.

We look too much for comfort. We need to be startled and surprised more often, and to open ourselves to adventure.

We need to choose to live more fully—to try new foods, meet new people, go to new places, read new books and explore new territory. We need to let freshness open up our lives and minds, no matter how uncomfortable it makes us.

I was thinking of all this on the beach at La Jolla as I watched a man dragging handfuls of sand out of the ocean for his kids to see.

He, the two youngsters and his wife went painstakingly through each handful, exclaiming when they found a shell or sea animal.

The man was sunburned. He probably would have a terrible time sleeping that night. But he was having a great afternoon.

* * *

A woman told me recently that from the day she married her husband 10 years ago, she had been trying futilely to be close to his two sisters.

"They're nice to me," she said, "but they just don't seem to want to spend time with me like they do with each other. I had thought how great it would be to have sisters, because I never had one. But I realize now it's never going to happen."

Another woman told me she had always wanted her father to love her as much as he did her little sister.

"I would try so hard to make him love me, and then I would see him look at her, and he would have all this affection in his eyes that he never had when he looked at me. And it hurt.

"I've spent my whole life feeling bad about it and then about a year ago, I decided that I wasn't going to worry about it anymore. I know he isn't ever going to love me as much, and that's it."

She said that when she first faced it, she cried for hours, then she pretended she didn't care and was distant with her father.

"But I'm older and wiser now, and I have several children of my own. And I know that while you love all your kids, there are some you are just a little closer to. When I stopped blaming my dad and expecting him to be different, I could appreciate him for the love and support he has given me and not expect more."

Both women had realized that there are times in your life when you have to accept the reality of a situation. And once you do, you discover a reward: It's easier to live with the situation than it was when you were fighting it.

For instance, you may have to accept the fact that your husband is going to favor his children over your children from another marriage. It may not make the children feel any better, but it will ease the tension between you if you're not trying to change something you can't change anyway.

While we don't like to accept it, it is nearly impossible to make someone love someone else the way you think they should. Feelings are not that easily manipulated.

So you may have to accept that your mother and father-in-law are never going to like you. Just try to ease the tension by trying not to see them too often and by being as nice as possible to them when you do.

When you quit wishing for something you don't have, you can concentrate on the things you have. You may often find that denial of the situation was harder on you than facing reality.

One mother told me she worried for years because her mother obviously favored her grandson over her granddaughter. She could see the hurt in her daughter's face when the grandmother ignored her and concentrated on the boy.

When the daughter was about 16, the mother talked with her about her grandmother. The girl was relieved to find it wasn't her imagination that Grandma seemed to love her brother better. And it helped to have her mother explain that it wasn't her fault—that she wasn't less lovable than her brother because Grandma was nicer to him.

As her mother talked, the girl nodded solemnly, crying softly. Then suddenly she brightened.

"That's OK," she said. "He doesn't show it that much, but I've always known Grandpa loves ME best."

* * *

Pleasure.

Our lives are so full of it.

Usually in ways so small, we hardly notice them.

We move from pleasure to pleasure each day. Sunlight on the breakfast table. A cup of coffee with the morning paper. A song on the radio. A talk with a friend. A phone call from a brother. Late sun on the mountains, softening the afternoon into evening. A long shower, a longer tub bath. A clean bed.

The feel of a baby in your arms and against your cheek. A loved one's back to cuddle up to and slip your arms around.

And these pleasurable things abound in the midst of trouble. A woman manager leaves problems at work and finds enjoyment in the fact that the fish in her pond had babies.

A family facing a financial crisis had friends over for volleyball and then sat laughing and talking late into the coolness of a fall night.

They could laugh in the face of disaster, explained

the man, because "I decided that for one evening I wasn't going to worry about it. I just wanted to enjoy myself for a change."

Ah, there is the difficulty. Most of us just can't decide not to worry. Even when pleasure abounds, even when we're in the midst of it, we deny it to ourselves.

As we're listening to one of our favorite songs, we're worrying about the speech we have to give tomorrow. As we're talking on the telephone to a friend, we're worried about the chores that might not get done.

When the breeze blows softly and the sunset beckons us to an evening walk, we say no to its invitation because we've got to get to bed early—it's a big day tomorrow.

We simply aren't comfortable allowing ourselves to enjoy the offerings of the moment. We're too concerned with what we have to do the next moment or what we did wrong the last moment.

Once in awhile, I will get a day or two when I can get away from worry enough to relish each tiny thing that happens. Last weekend was one of those times.

I enjoyed everything from the silky feel of a favorite blouse to the laughter in a nephew's dark eyes as we sat talking. I allowed myself the luxury of lying and listening to music—not getting chores done while it was on—but just relaxing into the rhythm and melody.

I let myself sit for more than an hour on a bench by myself at a friend's farmhouse, and I didn't feel a bit guilty as I gazed at the colors of the mountains, felt the coolness of the morning breeze and watched the shadows of the trees make patterns on the grass.

It's interesting. Despite all this self-indulgence, I got just as much done as on most other weekends.

The difference was, I was happier.

* * *

They had planned the weekend trip to the mountains for months, and the morning was as sunny as her mood as they drove toward the freeway and freedom from the hassles of the city.

Unfortunately, they didn't escape the hassles soon enough. Shortly after getting on the freeway, a car in another lane jumped in front of them, causing her husband to swerve slightly and squeal the brakes to avoid him.

He swore, and the next thing she knew, he was trying to get even. He pulled into the outer lane and sped up to get into position to duck in front of the man who had ducked in front of him.

"What are you doing?" she said. "This is stupid!"

Her husband set his mouth and chin and slowed down to a crawl. She knew him well enough to realize he was now mad at three people: at the other driver, at her for yelling at him and at himself because he hated it when his temper flared and he reacted irrationally.

She also knew that he was going to be mad for several hours, at least, or the whole weekend, at most. After tolerating an hour of his silent and grim concentration on driving, she remarked:

"You know, that other driver has completely forgotten this whole episode. He would be tickled to death to know he's causing you this much misery. I think it's silly to let some stupid guy ruin your trip, and he's not bothered a bit!"

As he set his jaw tighter and didn't respond, she made up her mind to be quiet and let him get over it. She also decided to try something she had been learning to do more lately.

In the past, she would have sat next to him, furious that he was not only ruining his trip but her own by his ridiculous anger. Involved in her own self-righteous indignation, she would have missed the beautiful scenery they were passing through and been unable to enjoy anything until he was through his mood and able to enjoy it with her again.

But this time, she said to herself, "He has a right to his anger, to his mood. He can make that choice, if he likes. But I have a right to choose my mood, too, and I can choose not to let him bother me. I can choose to enjoy the scenery and have a good time and let him have the time, too, to work things through without nagging him about it."

It worked. Even though he remained glum as he drove, she found herself reveling in the sunlight on meadows and the sweet scent of pine in the air as they traveled higher in the mountains.

Several hours later, they stopped to eat at a quaint restaurant, and her husband, his anger past, was soon enjoying the meal, joking with the waitress and generally having a good time. The rest of the weekend was a shared pleasure for both of them.

"I learned something," she told a friend later. "First of all, I think he got over the mood faster because I didn't get angry at him and make him more defensive.

"After all, if you think about it, outside of insisting he not jeopardize my safety by ducking in front of the other guy, it's unfair of me to require him to handle things differently than he feels he needs to. If he needs hours to work through things, then that's what he needs.

"But what I really discovered was I can be in charge of my own happiness. I CAN decide not to let someone else's bad mood ruin my day. I can decide to have a good time almost any time I want to."

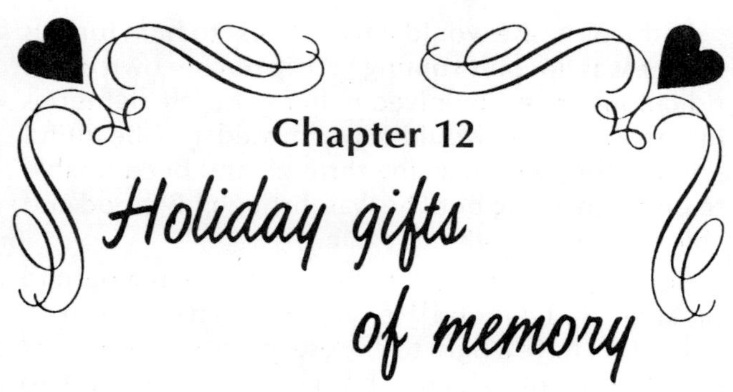

Chapter 12
Holiday gifts of memory

Easter, with its theme of resurrection, reminds me of the indestructibility of the human spirit—of the hidden something inside human beings that survives the death of dreams and urges us on to dream again.

If you doubt it, look back on your own life. Chances are you have struggled through several crises to find that happiness exists on the other side of hopelessness.

Perhaps your marriage was falling apart, and you were certain you and your mate would never be able to bridge the chasms you had created with angry words and thoughtless acts. But then, because you both were willing to give anything to make it work, you made it, and now you're advising your children about getting through the hard times.

Or perhaps when you were young, you thought you would never find someone to love, but you did. And he or she was better than you had hoped for.

Or perhaps there were months when you thought you would never get over divorce, would never love again, would never be happy again. But you found new life, first in freedom and your own strength and then in a new love.

And what about those years when you thought you would never get through those rough times with your teenage son or daughter? Even if you both survived their adolescence, you knew your relationship would never be whole and loving again. Now, a short time later, your adult child and you are the best of friends.

Think of the year you lost your job and were certain you'd never get another. But after months of humiliating interviews and applications that headed only for the wastebasket, you found another job, better-paying and more satisfying than the one you lost.

Or remember the day you didn't get the promotion you wanted, and you felt you were at a dead end in your profession, that the last opportunity had passed you by. A few months later, another opportunity arose, and this time you got the new office and the new challenges.

Think of all the dreams you've realized that you thought you never would or the problems you've solved that you thought you couldn't:

The home you thought you could never afford that is now yours.

The child you thought you'd never have but is now 7 going on 8.

The trip to Europe you always dreamed of but couldn't imagine ever taking, but you just picked up your passport for this summer.

The friend you thought you had alienated forever but who called to take you out to dinner last week.

The pain you were told would never go away, but the doctor gave you a prescription for a new medicine and you feel better than you have in years.

The book or song or painting you thought no one would ever buy, but they did.

The business you started when everyone said you'd never make it, but you did.

And, of course, most families have stories of miraculous comebacks: relatives who survived serious accidents unscathed; loved ones who "died" for a while, only to come back and talk of it.

Most of us have lost loved ones, and you probably have known times in your life when you were so deeply despairing that you thought of suicide. But something strong and sustaining inside you refused to give up, so you lived to laugh and love again.

On this Easter morning, aren't you glad you did?

* * *

What fun I had when I was a kid putting together a costume for Halloween from all the remnants of past Halloweens and past family experiences that were tucked away in my mother's ever-growing collection of cardboard boxes.

What did I feel like being this holiday? Would I be a princess, beautiful and elegant in a dress of old lace curtains, Christmas tinsel crown and an aunt's castoff high-heel shoes? Or would I be a fat tramp in my father's old pants and shoes, carrying a handkerchief bundle on a stick?

Or would I be a ghost, hiding my face and body comfortably under one of Mama's old sheets? Or did I want to be a witch, winning fearful respect of little kids with my threatening face and laugh?

I think what costume we choose tells a lot about us. When I look at my costume choices, each one said something about my personality at the time. Part of me wanted to be the princess, beautiful and admired and pampered by a prince. Part of me wanted to be the witch, inspiring awe in others, having control over all aspects of my life instead of having to live with the control of parent, teacher and peer approval.

Part of me wanted to hide under a sheet of

anonymity, losing myself in reading and writing, watching the world go by from a hidden corner window. And part of me wanted to be the funny tramp, unconcerned about my appearance, unconcerned about the responsibility of making good grades or doing my share of the housework. That part just wanted to have fun.

If costumes do reflect our secret desires, what would you choose? I would have chosen different ones at different times of my life.

When I was 10 and sickly I would have chosen the costume of the athlete. It would have been great, for instance, to be like my younger sister whose grammar school coach still remarks about what a great softball player she was. It would have been nice to be the first chosen for every team, instead of the last.

When I was 15, I would have chosen a cheerleader costume. I would have been bouncy, little, fun and beautiful and outgoing, instead of tall, skinny, shy and uncomfortable at parties and on the dance floor.

When I was a young mother, I would have chosen the neatly washed and perfectly pressed apron of the ideal wife and mother. I would have been Donna Reed's double, with my table always perfectly set and husband always beaming on me as I made life go right for him and my ever-smiling, well-behaved children.

But life decreed I wasn't to be stay-at-home Donna Reed; I was a career woman. So, as a journalist, I would have chosen the overcoat and pulled-down hat of the investigative reporter. I would ferret out evils in the shadows of government offices and business buildings, and receive the accolades of my peers and public for my hard-hitting articles about crime and corruption.

But that costume didn't fit me either. I was always more comfortable writing about Christmas than crime.

I was always happier finding the good things in people than looking for the bad.

I've accepted that the investigative cloak will never be my costume, but I still vacillate between the costume of magazine-cover career woman, jean-clad hippie, and dramatic hostess to the world in colorful clothing and arty jewelry.

I guess my real goal is to be comfortable in my own skin each day, without worrying about costuming myself to please the world. I can be hippie some days, career woman others. I can be dramatic and a little outrageous whenever I feel like it. All are parts of me.

And I suspect my mother has a cardboard box with costumes for any part I decide to indulge today.

* * *

At Christmastime, I ride an emotional roller coaster. One minute I'm caught up in the joy of baking, making, shopping, wrapping—the next minute I'm looking forward to after the holidays, when I can go back to a more peaceful routine that includes some time just to think and dream.

One minute I'm thinking of the present, the next I'm wrapped in the past, the next I'm trying to peek into the future.

In the present I feel good about things, about the fullness of my life. Looking into the future, I feel an exhilaration about change and possibility, but also a fear of change and possibility. Will I get older and better, or just older?

Will I expand my life into wider circles of enjoyment and find deeper pools of serenity, as did my grandmother? Or will I end up like some of the lost people in a nursing home I just visited?

As for the past—when did we all become middle aged? When did my brothers stop matching spikes across the volleyball net at family gatherings and let their sons take their place? When did lines appear in my sisters' faces?

Wasn't it just yesterday that we were starting our lives with new houses, husbands and babies, hoping and planning and dreaming? When did our children take over the dreams?

I had a strong sense of passing the baton the other night, when my children and I decorated the Christmas tree.

My daughter and her husband are living in my home until they can afford their own. They like the space, the room for animals.

I like my apartment because I don't have to worry about things breaking down. Someday, I'll move back when the kids don't need the house; but for now, the apartment is my home.

So we went to buy the tree for the house, my son, my daughter and my son-in-law. This year they wouldn't let me pay. This year, my son and son-in-law carried it in and set it up. My daughter directed its placement.

I gave advice, and then wondered: Just last year, it seems, I was the one in charge. Now, I found myself stepping back. It was their tree, their house. I was no longer Mama running things, making things go right. They were making things go right without me.

In a house where they had been children, they were now adults. I found myself wanting to cry, right after I had been laughing about something funny or joyful or smiling at something tender that had passed among us.

We hung old ornaments on the tree. One was made of egg cartons and pieces of wrapping paper. It was bent with time, the only one left of several dozen I had made during my early years of marriage, when we had little money and a small tree that needed decorating. It was part of my children's babyhood. It will not survive many more Christmases.

My son's first-grade picture pasted on a styrofoam ball hung next to a tiny bear dangling from a string of bells. My daughter had just purchased that ornament and we commented that her children—my grandchildren—were going to love it someday.

Above it, a cage of tiny lovebirds proclaimed that it was my daughter's and her husband's first Christmas together. Past, present and future connected in the branches of a Christmas tree.

Perhaps the emotional undercurrent of the season is intensified because of the closeness of Christmas and New Year's Day. Christmas places emphasis on past family traditions, only to be followed by a new year and its urging to change and begin something new.

I know that life is change. I know that it is a constant process of synthesizing past and present, and taking what I learn into the future. I know that I should value each day's lessons, enjoy the pleasures and accept serenely that no moment can be held permanently.

Most of the year, I come closer to accepting that. But at Christmas, enveloped by memories of childish faces and younger dreams, I can't seem to escape the emotional ride.

* * *

Over the years, my grandmother maintained many Christmas traditions. She set up a tiny Christmas tree in the corner of her one-room apartment at my parents' house and around it placed the old dolls, animal figurines and stuffed animals she had collected over the years.

She bought and wrapped gifts for her children, grandchildren and the older women at church she knew wouldn't have much. She hung two favorite calendars for the coming year: Bill Keane's Family Circus calendar and one of cats with funny comments under them.

She perked the coffee for the family Christmas get-together the Saturday before Christmas, bringing in the pot as ceremoniously as Mrs. Cratchit brought in the plum pudding in **A Christmas Carol.** *And she always made cookies and candy for Christmas, wrapping them up in bright colors to give to her grandchildren.*

One Christmas, at least 10 years ago, Grandma tried a new recipe for cookies made with gumdrops. Of all the family, I loved them the most. So Grandma began making those cookies for me.

Even after she began to get too old to bake the number of cookies she used to, she still made the gumdrop ones for me, presenting them just as I was leaving the Christmas get-together to go home.

"Here's something for you," she would say, tucking it into my stack of packages, her eyes twinkling. Then we would hug each other, say "Merry Christmas" and I would eat gumdrop cookies all the way home.

A year ago August, Grandma died, and when last Christmas neared, I asked my mother for Grandma's cookie recipe. My grandmother had written it on a slip of white paper and at the top she noted: "Ginger's favorite."

I had the recipe laminated to save and put a copy in my recipe box, determined to continue Grandma's tradition by making the cookies myself for Christmas. But time went by too quickly, and when Christmas arrived, I had not made the cookies.

This year, I determined to do better. "I'm making

Grandma's cookies this year," I told my mother. "Even if I bake nothing else.'"

Of course, I couldn't bake "nothing else." My kids counted on their traditional sweets of divinity, popcorn balls, frosted sugar cookies and cheesy lemon squares. With work, seasonal parties, gift-buying and wrapping, it seemed I was never going to get my regular baking done, let alone find time to bake Grandma's cookies.

A few days ago, when my mother and I were wrapping gifts at my folks' home, I went out to Grandma's room to get some wrapping paper. The room, I thought sadly, was looking less and less like Grandma's room.

The corner that used to hold the Christmas tree was bare. Her bed had been moved out to make room for a double bed for company. Most of her keepsakes and furniture had gone to family members. Only a few pictures of grandchildren, taken years ago, hung from walls and sat on shelves where she had placed them.

I suddenly missed her terribly. And I resolved once again to make the cookies as if making them would somehow re-connect us.

As I left that night to go home, I hugged my mother goodbye, and she handed me a boxful of presents to put under my tree. One gift she handed to me separately.

"I want you to open this tonight when you get home," she said.

At home, I undid the red bow and removed the gold foil wrapping. Inside were my grandmother's gumdrop cookies, made for me by my mother—a bond of love reaching across three lives, across time.

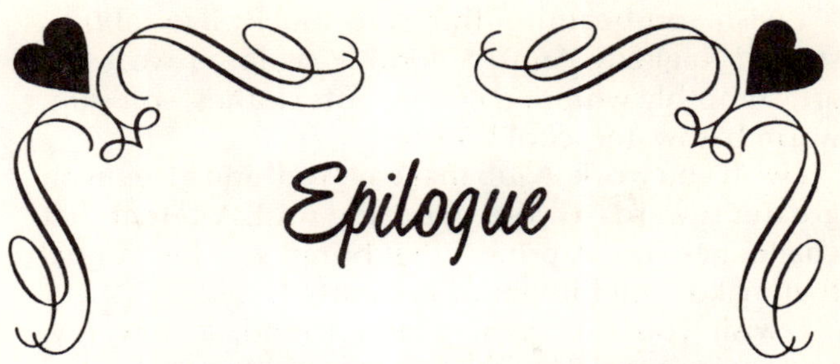

Epilogue

I wish you more things to enjoy this year. More good things to eat that will not make you fat. More fun things to do that will not get you in trouble.

I wish you people to love and love you. Good neighbors, good friends. Co-workers who put up with your idiosyncrasies, family members who do the same.

I wish you things to laugh at and about. More good jokes, more funny movies, more tolerance of your own foibles, your own mistakes.

I wish you reasons to get up: morning walks, morning coffee, morning newspaper. Sunrise.

I wish you reasons to go to sleep: soft pillows, soft beds, warm rooms, warm thoughts, sweet dreams.

I wish you beautiful things to see: flowers, starlit nights, mountain vistas unmarred by buildings, paintings and pictures. An act of friendship between strangers passing in the street. An expression of love between family members.

I wish you beautiful things to hear: symphonies of song, words and nature. Rain on the roof, wind at the window, birds and ocean waves. Someone saying you are wonderful.

I wish you beautiful things to smell: roses, rain on dust, a child's sun-warmed hair. Fresh air, fresh sheets and barbecuing steaks. New cars, new houses, new books, new leather jackets.

I wish you beautiful things to touch: live rabbits, stuffed Raggedy Anns. Smoothly sculpted works of art, smoothly whipped cream. Soft clothes, soft skin, warm bathwater, cool breezes.

I wish you work. A job that pays well and gives even greater rewards to your mind and soul. A career that challenges you. A project that brings you joy. A goal that makes you hunger to get started.

I wish you surprises: a new friend, a new toy. Something special in the mail, something unexpected in your Christmas stocking, something you wanted but dared not dream of in your life.

I wish you wisdom: right choices, right moves, insight, empathy. Anger when it is appropriate, acceptance when it is called for, understanding always.

I wish you discipline that comes easily and makes you feel good about yourself. A diet well done, a race well run. A new way of thinking, a new way of living.

I wish you a happier world. Less pollution of land, sea, air and conversation. Less worry, more hope. More love between neighbors and nations.

I wish you peace.